®VOGUEKNITTING
THE LEARN-TO-KNIT BOOK

VOGUEKNITTING
THE LEARN-TO-KNIT BOOK

THE EDITORS OF
VOGUE® KNITTING
MAGAZINE

sixth&springbooks

sixth&springbooks 104 West 27th Street, 3rd Floor
New York, NY 10001

Library of Congress Cataloging-in-Publication Data
Title: Vogue Knitting: The Learn-to-Knit Book / The editors of Vogue Knitting Magazine.
Other titles: Vogue Knitting International.
Description: First edition. | New York, NY : Sixth&Spring Books, 2020.
Includes index.

LCCN 2019033995 | ISBN 9781640210639
LCSH: Knitting. | Knitting--Patterns.
LCC TT820 .V6266 2020 | DDC 746.43/2041--dc23

LC record available at https://lccn.loc.gov/2019033995

Book and cover design by Diane Lamphron
Cover photography by Marcus Tullis

MANUFACTURED IN CHINA

FIRST EDITION

1 3 5 7 9 10 8 6 4 2

EDITOR-IN-CHIEF
Carla Scott

EDITOR
Pam Wissman

**ART DIRECTION
& DESIGN**
Diane Lamphron

KNITTER
Lori Steinberg

YARN EDITOR
Matthew Schrank

PHOTOGRAPHY
• STILL-LIFE
Pages 2, 3, 16, and all instruction photos:
MARCUS TULLIS

Pages 8–13:
JACK DEUTSCH

• FASHION PHOTOGRAPHY
Pages 89, 113 : Paul Amato for LVARepresents.com

Pages 66–69, 72–73, 75, 91, 103, 105, 107, 111, 121:
ROSE CALLAHAN

Pages 70–73, 77, 81–87, 93, 95, 97-101, 107, 114–119, 122–126:
JACK DEUTSCH
Page 79: Kip Meyer
Page 109: Marco Zambelli

**CHIEF EXECUTIVE
OFFICER**
Caroline Kilmer

PRESIDENT
Art Joinnides

CHAIRMAN
Jay Stein

FOLLOW US

 sixth&springbooks VOGUEKNITTING

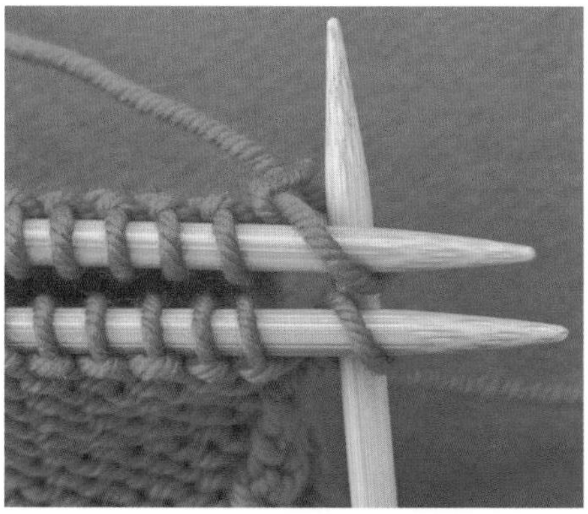
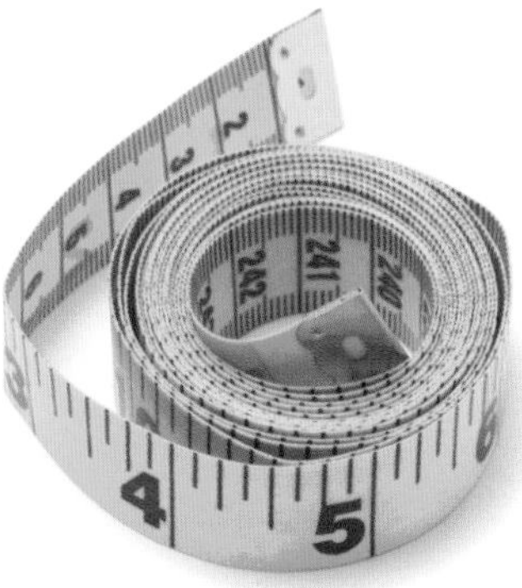
4
5
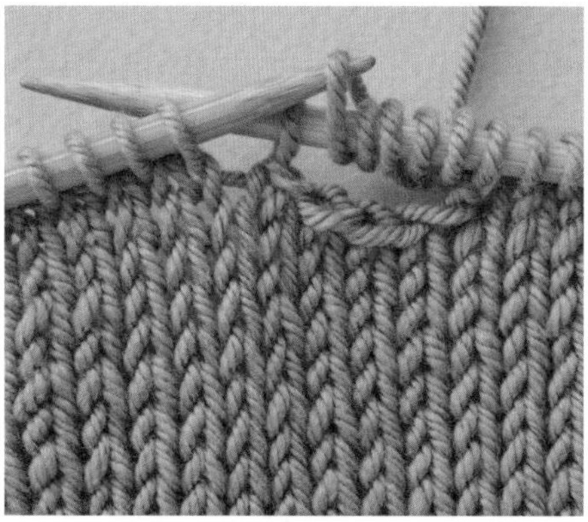
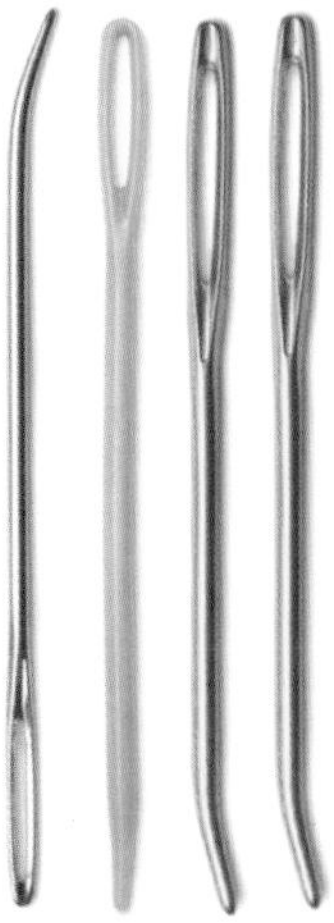
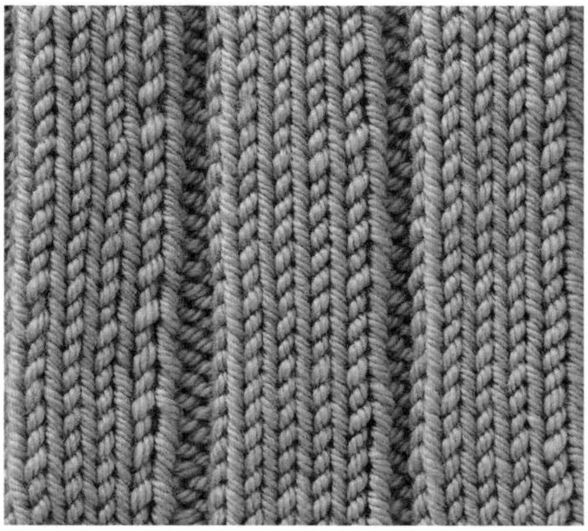
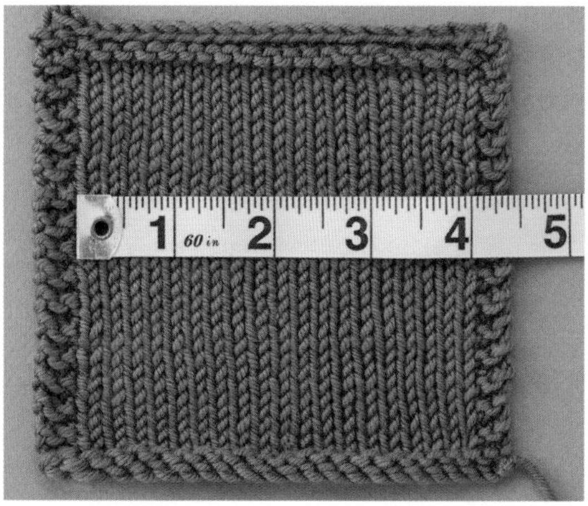
1 60 in 2 3 4 5
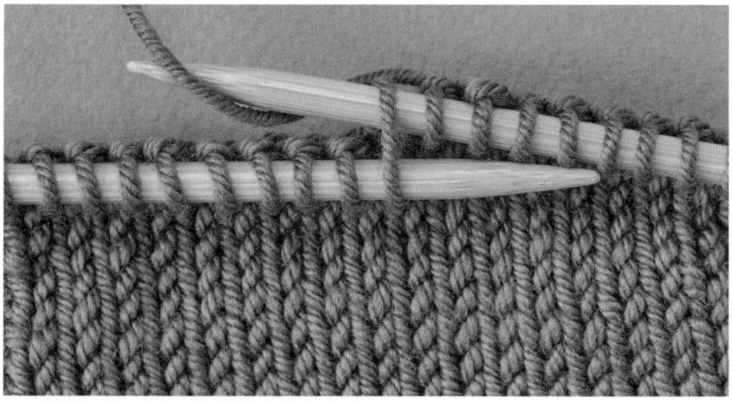
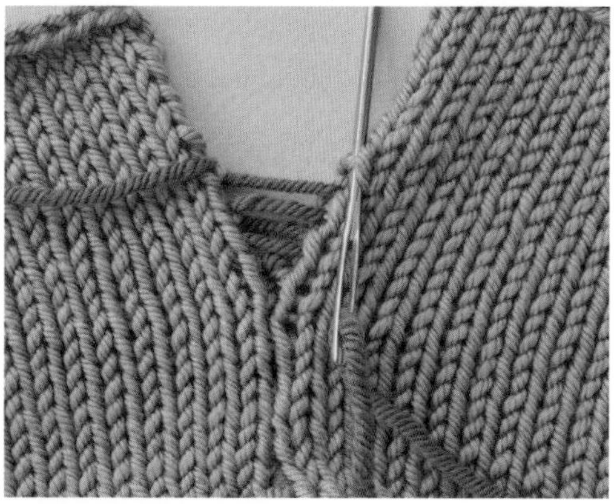
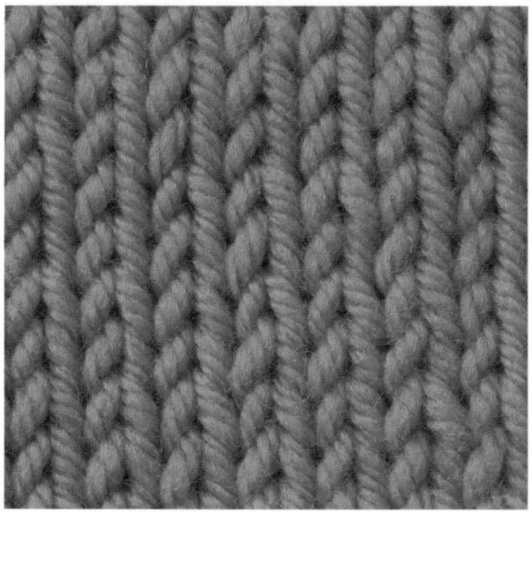
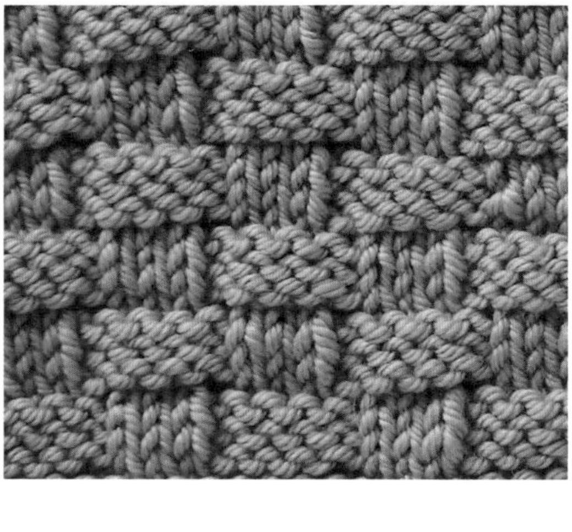
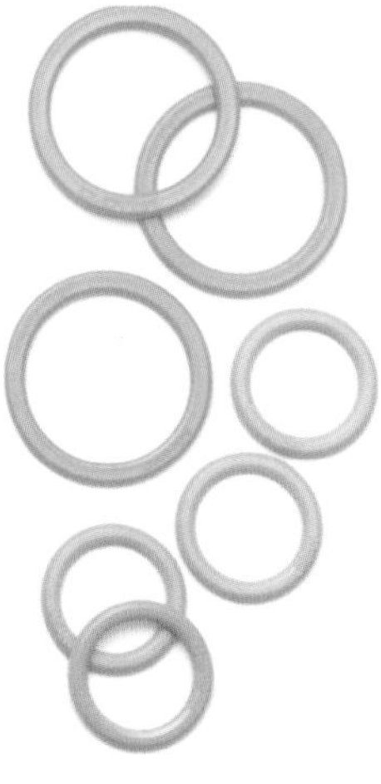
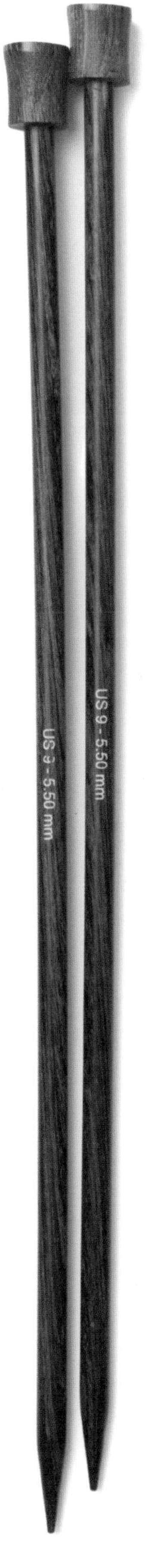
US 9 - 5.50 mm
US 9 - 5.50 mm

CONTENTS

3
A BASIC STITCH SAMPLER
41

4
FINISHING
53

5
SIMPLE PROJECTS
61

Learning to Knit

Knitting has timeless appeal. The same knitted stitches that date as far back as the 11th century are still practiced by a vibrant community of knitters today. Why does a craft that could have easily been made obsolete by machine-made knits have such staying power? As any knitter will tell you, knitting offers an abundance of benefits, whether it's the relaxing and meditative movement of the hands, the creative expression that is possible in each knitted project, or the satisfaction of making items that are both useful and beautiful. Ultimately, knitting is fulfilling—and fun!

Learning any new skill can seem daunting at first, but knitting is actually very simple. Just remember this: All knitting is made up of two basic stitches—the knit and the purl. Working with these stitches is as easy or as complicated as you choose to make it. You don't have to master the advanced aspects of knitting before you can create stunning garments and gifts that you will be proud to say you made by hand. This book will give you all the information you need to begin. Read on to discover more reasons to pick up a pair of knitting needles and yarn so you can start knitting now.

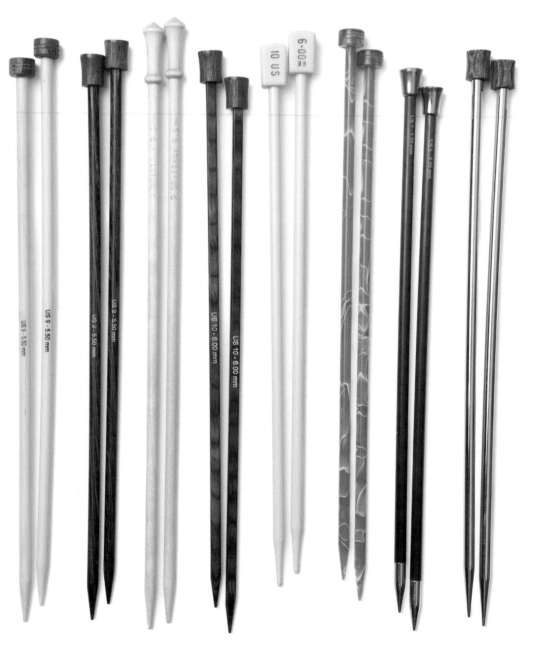

Getting Started

Start Exploring

Now that you know the benefits of learning to knit, it's time to join in the fun. Before you get started, you'll want to visit your local yarn shop or the yarn section of a craft store to get a feel for what's out there and to start gathering some supplies. Spend some time searching the internet for knitting-oriented websites. You can shop for just about anything without leaving your desk, but most knitters can't resist the visual, tactile, and social pleasures of the yarn-shop experience. When you visit your local yarn shop, introduce yourself as a new knitter. You'll be thrilled at the enthusiastic response—and this connection will come in handy later if you run into trouble and need some technical help.

Yarns

One of the most compelling reasons for taking up the craft of knitting is the abundance of fabulous knitting materials available from yarn shops, craft chains, and online suppliers.

CHOOSING YOUR FIRST YARN
In your excitement to start knitting, you may be eager to purchase textured novelty yarns, bulky yarns, and luxury fibers (like cashmere, angora, and alpaca). Be patient. We recommend learning with a basic

smooth yarn—it's easier to work with, doesn't split, and is more forgiving. And choose a light color—it's easier to see.

Yarn is organized by weight (thickness) and ranges from super-fine to super-bulky. For your first project, we recommend a worsted or mid-weight yarn. Nearly all yarn comes with a ball band or label clearly stating the recommended needle size and gauge. Always save the ball band as it is the source of lots more useful information, including fiber content and care

instructions (see below). Most commercial yarn you'll run across will be in the form of a ball (round) or skein (oblong), with the yarn pulling out from the center. You might find a yarn you love that's "put up" in hank form, which will have to be wound into a ball. If the yarn shop can't do that for you, enlist a friend (or kid) to act as a human swift while you wind the ball.

HOW TO READ A YARN LABEL
Knowing how to read the basic elements of a yarn label will help you choose the right yarn and needles for your projects.

1. YARN WEIGHT	6. FIBER
2. ORIGIN	7. PUT-UP/YARDAGE
3. CARE GUIDE	8. YARN NAME
4. GAUGE	9. YARN COMPANY
5. NEEDLE SIZE	10. COLOR & DYE LOT

TYPES OF YARN

The fiber and texture choices out there are pretty staggering, but fun to explore. Let's start with your traditional worsteds. These smooth, medium-weight yarns are the classic choice for sweaters; they make stitch patterns stand out and are generally the easiest for beginners to work with. Then there are the fuzzy, textured yarns like angora, mohair, bouclé (which looks like little curlicues), and chenille. You'll find them in all-natural wool, cashmere, cotton, alpaca, and other animal or plant fibers; acrylic and nylon; or blends of two or more fibers. These give lots of texture but can be a bit trickier to knit with since it's harder to see your stitches. Next are the novelties, such as faux fur, eyelash, twist, and combination yarns. These are great for making something incredibly simple (a garter-stitch scarf, for instance) look totally special. We also like them for accents on collars and cuffs. Like textured yarns, novelty yarns make it a bit tricky to see stitches, but they also hide a multitude of beginner mistakes.

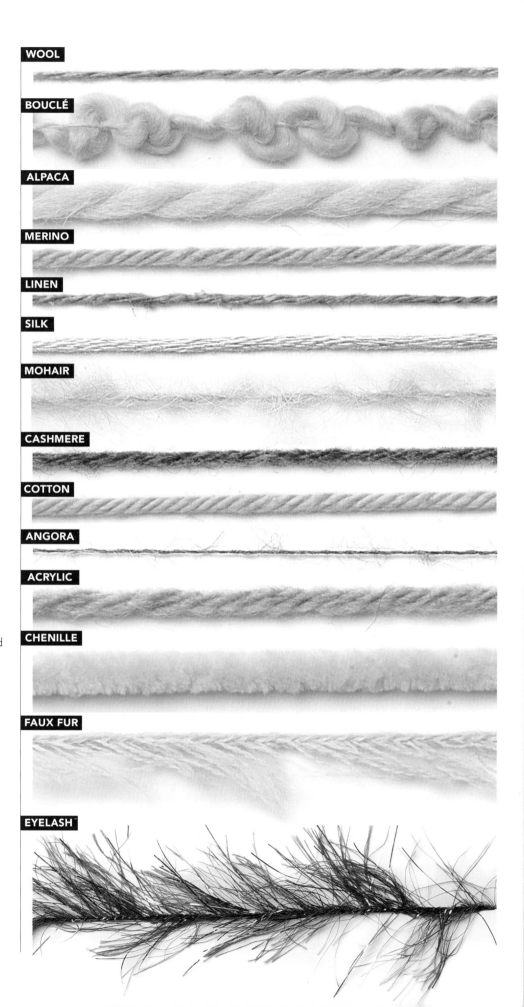

WOOL

BOUCLÉ

ALPACA

MERINO

LINEN

SILK

MOHAIR

CASHMERE

COTTON

ANGORA

ACRYLIC

CHENILLE

FAUX FUR

EYELASH

YARN WEIGHTS

No matter the fiber content, all yarns are grouped into basic categories (fingering, sport, DK, worsted, bulky, etc.) designed to help you pick the right one for your project—and your needle size. Weight (the thickness of the yarn) is the measure by which all yarns are judged, and the industry has come up with a standardized list of symbols and terms to help you identify it. For the most part you'll use thinner yarns on smaller needles and thicker yarns on bigger needles. Check the yarn label for the standardized weight symbols and information.

STANDARD YARN WEIGHTS

Yarn Weight Symbol & Category Names	0 Lace	1 Super Fine	2 Fine	3 Light weight	4 Medium	5 Bulky	6 Super Bulky	7 Jumbo
Type of Yarns in Category	Fingering 10-count crochet thread	Sock, Fingering, Baby	Sport, Baby	DK, Light Worsted	Worsted, Afghan, Aran	Chunky, Craft, Rug	Super Bulky, Roving	Jumbo, Roving
Knit Gauge Range* in Stockinette Stitch to 4 inches	33–40** sts	27–32 sts	23–26 sts	21–24 sts	16–20 sts	12–15 sts	7–11 sts	6 sts and fewer
Recommended Needle in Metric Size Range	1.5–2.25mm	2.25–3.25mm	3.25–3.75mm	3.75–4.5mm	4.5–5.5mm	5.5–8mm	8–12.75mm	12.75mm and larger
Recommended Needle in U.S. Size Range	000–1	1–3	3–5	5–7	7–9	9–11	11–17	17 and larger

* GUIDELINES ONLY: The above reflect the most commonly used gauges and needle sizes for specific yarn categories.
** Lace-weight yarns are usually knitted on larger needles to create lacy, openwork patterns. Accordingly, a gauge range is difficult to determine. Always follow the gauge stated in your pattern.

Needles

Knitting needles come in a wide variety of materials. Traditional metal needles can help the yarn easily slide from the needle for fast knitting. Plastic needles are lightweight and widely available. A popular choice for many knitters is wood or bamboo needles, which have a warm, earthy feel to them and rounded ends that don't split the yarn. Bamboo is flexible and the needles warm up as you work with them. Wooden needles, available in everything from birch to ebony, are elegant to the eye and pleasing to the touch but tend to be pricey. It's a good idea to experiment and see which material feels most comfortable to you.

Knitting needles range in thickness from very thin (for making socks or fine lace) to extremely thick (for working with mega-bulky yarns). The size of the needle corresponds with the size of the yarn and the recommended needle size is indicated on the yarn's label.

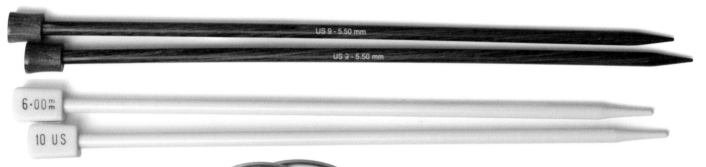

STRAIGHT NEEDLES

Straight needles are the long, straight single-pointed needles that are most commonly associated with knitting. They have a point on one end and a knob on the other that keeps your stitches from sliding off the needle. Straight needles are sold in pairs of various lengths, with 10" (25cm) and 14" (35cm) being the most common. They'll get you through the majority of the projects you encounter.

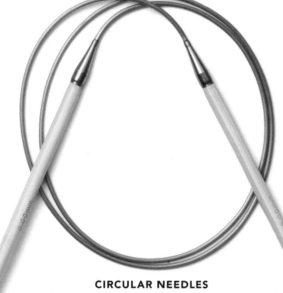

CIRCULAR NEEDLES

Circular needles are made with two shorter pointed needles attached to one another with a length of smooth nylon cord. You can use them to knit tubular pieces (leg warmers, hats, seamless sweaters) or flat pieces.

DOUBLE-POINTED NEEDLES

Double-pointed needles (dpns) have points on both ends and are used to make small items in the round, turn sock heels, or make I-cords. Cable needles are short with double points, and sometimes with a U shape in the center. They are used in cable knitting.

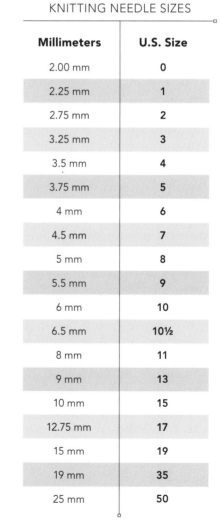

KNITTING NEEDLE SIZES

Millimeters	U.S. Size
2.00 mm	0
2.25 mm	1
2.75 mm	2
3.25 mm	3
3.5 mm	4
3.75 mm	5
4 mm	6
4.5 mm	7
5 mm	8
5.5 mm	9
6 mm	10
6.5 mm	10½
8 mm	11
9 mm	13
10 mm	15
12.75 mm	17
15 mm	19
19 mm	35
25 mm	50

Beyond yarn and an assortment of needles, you'll need a few other tools and accessories to get started. Some are more essential than others; we've broken the list down into the must-haves (A-List) and the nice-to-haves (B-List).

THE A LIST
SCISSORS
Whether you stick to a strictly utilitarian pair or splurge on a more decorative design, you'll need these to cut yarn, make fringe and snip off loose ends. Pick a small pair with a sharp point that allows you to get close to the work. If you'll be doing a lot of knitting on the go, get a sleeve that protects the point or slip the scissors into a little zippered pouch so they won't poke holes in your bag—or cut your fingers when you reach in to grab them.

YARN NEEDLES
Sometimes called tapestry needles, these have a blunt point and a wide eye (that's the little hole at the top of the needle) to accommodate thick yarn. You'll need these to sew seams and weave in ends. Both the metal and colorful plastic styles available work equally well.

TAPE MEASURE
A tape measure is essential. Your basic yellow dressmaker's tape will do just fine, but many interesting, retractable styles exist that make measuring a little more fun. Just be sure the tape is marked in both inches and centimeters and is made of fiberglass, since cloth tends to stretch.

RULER OR STITCH GAUGE
One or the other is essential for checking the ever-important knitting gauge. Rulers work just fine, but stitch gauges have neat little windows that make it easier to count the number of stitches and rows. Some even have a row of holes you can use to identify the size of unmarked needles. You'll learn more about gauge later.

PINS
You'll need pins for seaming and blocking. You'll want a good stock of long, straight, rustproof pins with glass or metal heads (plastic can melt under the heat of your iron) and T-pins for blocking. You can also purchase special blocking pins that are longer and more flexible than traditional T-pins.

CROCHET HOOK
Every knitter needs at least one hook to help pick up stitches, make decorative edgings and seam slip stitches.

STITCH HOLDERS
Slip open stitches (like those on a neckline) onto these oversized safety pins to keep them from unraveling until you are ready to pick them up again.

STITCH MARKERS
These little plastic or metal rings are handy for keeping track of things like where to increase and decrease or the beginning of a circular row. Split markers have a little slit in the ring so you can slip the marker into the stitches instead of over the needle.

THE B LIST
These aren't essential, but they will make your knitting life easier.

POMPOM MAKERS
These little plastic disks work like magic to create perfectly plush and perky pompoms. Follow the directions on the package to get the best results.

POINT PROTECTORS
These are little rubber-pointed covers you put over the points of your needles to keep stitches from falling off. They also prevent needles from poking holes in your bag. They are available in lots of sizes, shapes, and colors.

BOBBINS
When you do colorwork, wind yarn around these little plastic holders, using them like small-scale balls of yarn. They help prevent tangles and make it easier to work the design.

NEEDLE CASES
Like knitting bags, these little accessories have exploded in style and popularity. Some are simple plastic zippered cases, others are artfully designed rolls crafted from silk or other fabrics. Look for one with loops to hold hooks and needles and a flap or zippered closure to keep them from spilling out.

NOTEBOOK
It's a good idea to keep a record of what you've made and how you did it. You can use a simple spiral-bound notebook to keep track of your progress or splurge on one of the many knitting journals offering space to record everything from yarn and needle inventories to your thoughts on what you're knitting and why you're knitting it.

GOOD TO KNOW

ALTER-KNIT TOOLS
Caught short without the tool you need? Try these substitutes.

STITCH HOLDER
Thread stitches onto a length of yarn or cording and tie the ends.

POINT PROTECTORS
Push the needle tips into erasers or wrap rubber bands around the points.

CABLE NEEDLE
A skinny pencil makes a nice substitute; just take care that yarn doesn't snag on the metal that holds the eraser.

STITCH MARKERS
Tie short pieces of yarn into little loops and slip over your needles (a contrasting color will work best).

KNITTING TOTE
Is this an essential? Probably. You'll need a spot for storing your stuff, and while your old backpack or a plastic grocery sack will do the job just fine, it's kind of nice to have a beautiful bag to tote around town. The best knitting totes have multiple pockets for needles and accessories and offer easy access to your work-in-progress.

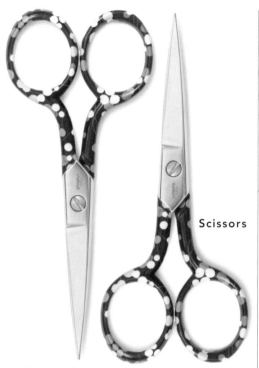
Scissors

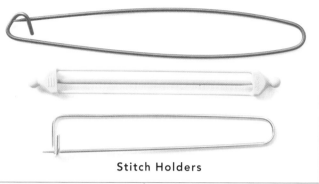
Stitch Holders

Crochet Hooks

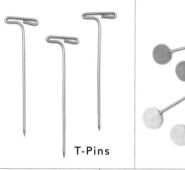
T-Pins

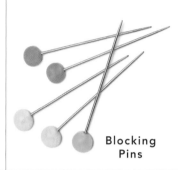
Blocking Pins

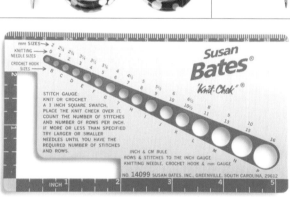
Stitch Gauge

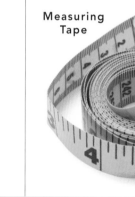
Measuring Tape

Stitch Markers

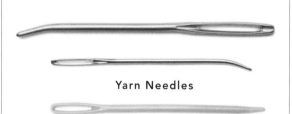
Yarn Needles

Point Protectors

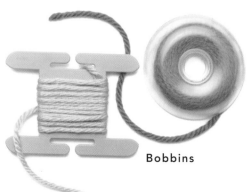
Bobbins

Pompom Makers

Notebook

ORGANIZING

Once you have a few knitting projects underway, you'll undoubtedly realize you need a system for organizing your yarn stash. One way is to initiate the "tote bag system" of organization—a separate bag for each project you've begun, containing yarn (don't forget to save the ball bands), needles, and the pattern you are using. Keep your pattern in a plastic sleeve for protection as you knit. When you're done with the project, insert the pattern into a loose-leaf binder or knitting notebook along with other information pertaining to that project—yarn ball bands, a note of where you bought the yarn, and a snapshot of the recipient. You'll be able to look back and see what you made and for whom. Many knitting shops sell a variety of knitter's journals designed especially for keeping a record of completed projects. Store needles in a needle holder, organized by size.

Holding the Yarn: English and Continental

One of the most important things for a new knitter of any age is finding the most comfortable way to hold the yarn and needles. With just a little time and patience, your hands will fall into a comfortable rhythm. The two main styles of knitting are English and Continental. Though both create the same end product, most knitters have very specific opinions about which way is better. Here's the major difference: English knitters hold and "throw" the yarn with their right hand, while Continental knitters manipulate the yarn with their left hand. This book will show you how to create the basic knit and purl stitches using both methods.

Once you've decided which hand will hold the working yarn, there's still one more decision to make—how to hold the needles. Some knitters like to grasp their needles over the top, while others would rather hold them like pencils, resting the majority of the needles between the thumb and index finger. There is honestly no right or wrong way to accomplish this, so experiment with the different choices. You will soon develop your own unique style.

Be prepared for a little awkwardness in the beginning. Give yourself plenty of time to get comfortable with the new hand positions and motions involved in knitting. With a little time and patience, you will be knitting with ease!

Casting On

There are many ways to get those initial stitches on the needle. We have selected two of the simplest, most sturdy, and neatly attractive versions to start with. The first, a double cast-on (also known as a long-tail cast-on), uses one needle and two lengths of yarn. Our second method, the knit-on cast-on, uses two needles and one strand.

A solid cast-on row leads to good results. The best way to perfect this method is to practice casting on, using your favorite method or technique, until it becomes an easy process for you.

It's possible that when you first start to cast on, your foundation row will be so tight that it will be tricky to get your needle through those little loops. If you have this problem, try casting on with two needles held together or using a needle two sizes larger than you'll be using for the remainder of the project.

SLIPKNOT

The slipknot is the beginning of the process—it anchors the yarn to the needles and makes casting on possible. Before you begin the slipknot, decide which method of casting on to try. For the double cast-on method, leave about an inch of yarn for every stitch that you want to place on the needle. If you choose the knit-on cast-on method, leave eight to ten inches between the end of the yarn and the slipknot.

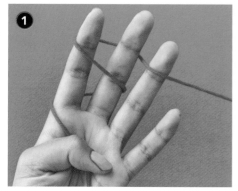

1. Hold the short end of the yarn in your palm with your thumb. Wrap the yarn twice around the index and middle fingers.

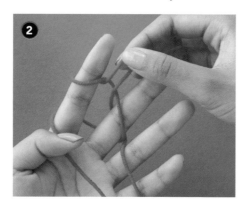

2. Pull the strand attached to the ball through the loop between your two fingers, forming a new loop.

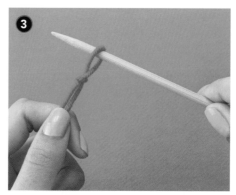

3. Place the new loop on the needle. Tighten the loop on the needle by pulling on both ends of the yarn to form the slipknot. You are now ready to begin casting on. ∎

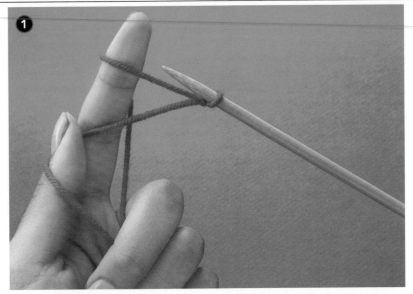

1. Make a slipknot on the right needle, leaving a long tail. Wind the tail-end around your left thumb, front to back. Wrap the yarn from the ball over your left index finger and secure the ends in your palm.

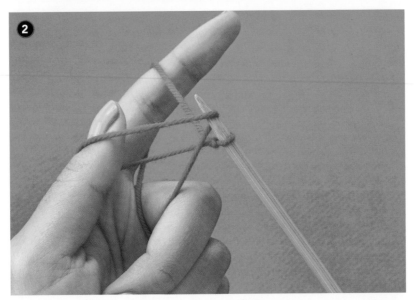

2. Insert the needle from front to back, upward in the loop on your thumb.

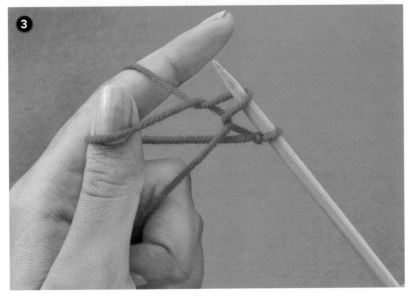

3. With the needle, draw the yarn from the ball through the loop to form a stitch. Take your thumb out of the loop and tighten the loop on the needle. Continue in this way until all the stitches are cast on. ∎

1. Make a slipknot on the left needle. *Insert the right needle knitwise into the stitch on the left needle. Wrap the yarn around the right needle as if to knit.

2. Draw the yarn through the first stitch to make a new stitch, but do not drop the first stitch from the left needle.

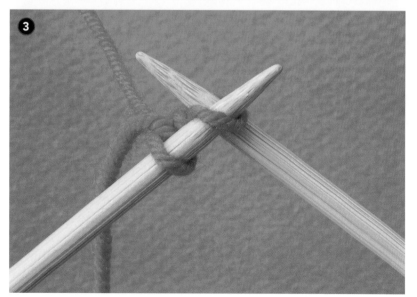

3. Slip the new stitch to the left needle as shown. Repeat from the * (in step 1) until the required number of stitches is cast on. ∎

After you're comfortable with casting on, you can begin knitting. There are two different ways to make each knit stitch: the English method or the Continental method. Try both and use whichever one feels most comfortable.

It may take some time to feel at ease, but keep practicing and soon the knit stitch will feel natural. The first row after the cast-on row is the most difficult. A friend who is an experienced knitter can help make the learning process easier.

KNIT STITCH: ENGLISH

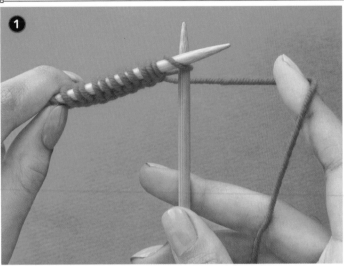

1. Hold the needle with the cast-on stitches in your left hand. Hold the working needle in your right hand, wrapping the yarn around your fingers. Insert the right needle from front to back into the first cast-on stitch on the left needle. Keep the right needle under the left needle and the yarn at the back.

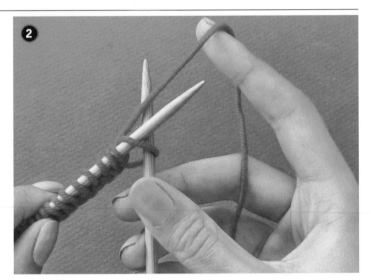

2. Wrap the yarn under and over the right needle in a clockwise motion.

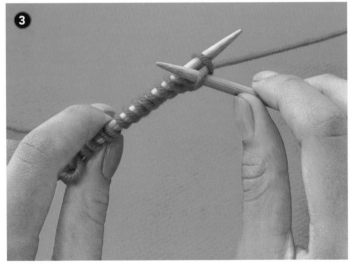

3. With the right needle, catch the yarn and pull it through the cast-on stitch.

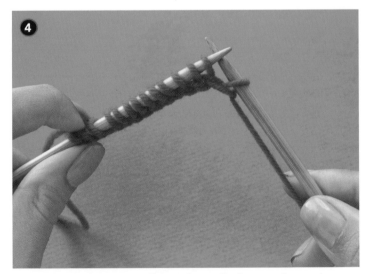

4. Slip the cast-on stitch off the left needle, leaving the newly formed stitch on the right needle. Repeat these steps in each subsequent stitch until all stitches have been worked from the left needle. You have made one row of knit stitches. ■

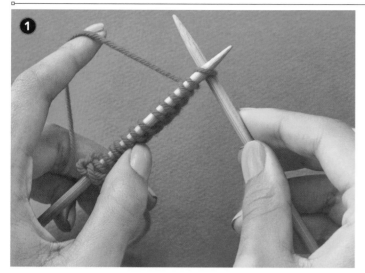

1. Hold the needles in the same way as the English method, but hold the yarn with your left hand rather than your right. Insert the right needle from front to back into the first cast-on stitch on the left needle. Keep the right needle under the left needle, with the yarn at the back.

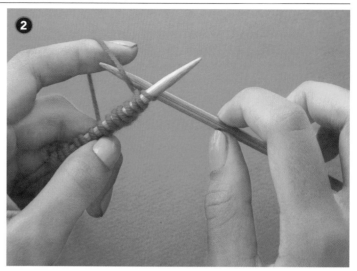

2. Lay the yarn over the right needle as shown.

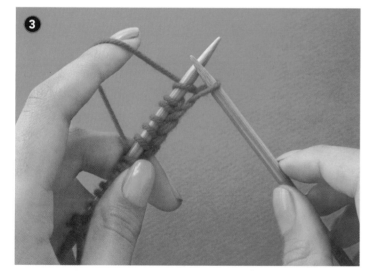

3. With the tip of the right needle, pull the strand through the cast-on stitch, holding the strand with the right index finger if necessary.

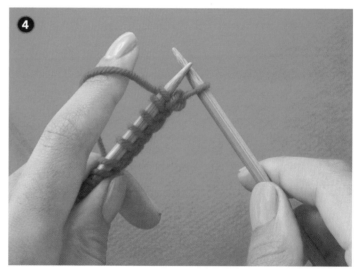

4. Slip the cast-on stitch off the left needle, leaving the newly formed stitch on the right needle. Continue to repeat these steps until you have worked all of the stitches from the left needle to the right needle. You have made one row of knit stitches. ■

GARTER STITCH

The garter stitch is the simplest of all stitch patterns and is completed by knitting every row. The end result will be a flat, reversible, ridged fabric that will stand up well to wear and will not roll at the edges.

After you reach the end of the first row of knit stitches, move the full needle to your left hand and begin knitting each stitch all over again. Once you have completed several rows, you'll start to see the results. As you get deeper into the project, your growing strip of garter stitch will begin to look like a real piece of knitted fabric.

Purl Stitch

The next, and equally important stitch is the purl stitch. In reality, purling is just the reverse version of knitting. When you put knitting and purling together, you can come up with literally hundreds of stitch patterns.

PURL STITCH: ENGLISH

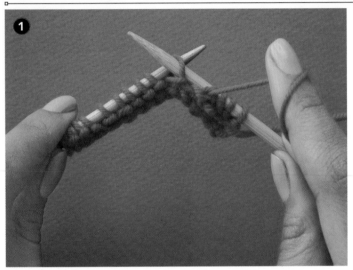

1. As with the knit stitch, hold the working needle in your right hand and the needle with the stitches in your left. The yarn is held and manipulated with your right hand and is kept to the front of the work. Insert the right needle from back to front into the first stitch on the left needle. The right needle is now in front of the left needle, and the yarn is at the front of the work.

2. With your right index finger, wrap the yarn counterclockwise around the right needle.

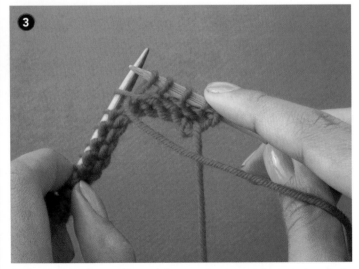

3. Draw the right needle and the yarn backward through the stitch on the left needle, forming a loop on the right needle.

4. Slip the stitch off the left needle. You have made one purl stitch. Repeat these steps in each subsequent stitch until all stitches have been worked from the left needle. You have made one row of purl stitches. ■

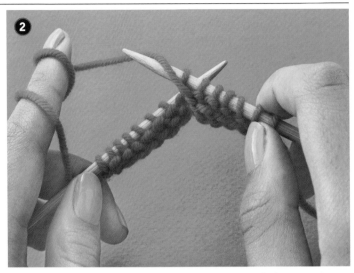

1. As with the knit stitch, hold the working needle in your right hand and the needle with the stitches in your left. The yarn is held and manipulated with your left hand and is kept to the front of the work. Insert the right needle from back to front into the first stitch on the left needle, keeping the yarn in front of the work.

2. Lay the yarn over the right needle as shown. Pull down on the yarn with your left index finger to keep the yarn taut.

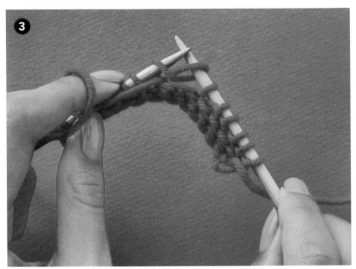

3. Bring the right needle and the yarn backward through the stitch on the left needle, forming a loop on the right needle.

4. Slide the stitch off the left needle. Use your left index finger to tighten the new purl stitch on the right needle. Continue to repeat these steps until you have worked all of the stitches from the left needle to the right needle. You have made one row of purl stitches. ∎

STOCKINETTE STITCH

Knit and purl stitches can be combined to create stockinette stitch, the beautiful V-patterned fabric that people most often associate with knitting. It is created by alternating rows of knitting and purling.

After you are finished with your knitting, you will need to bind off your stitches so that your project will not unravel. Binding off is not complicated, but watch for tension. If you bind off too tightly, you will create a pucker on top. To prevent this, try binding off with a needle two sizes larger than you used for the rest of the project. If the instruction does not tell you how to bind off, assume that you will bind off from the right side and knitwise, as shown here.

1. Knit two stitches. *Insert the left needle from the front into the first stitch (the one further from the tip) on the right needle.

2. Pull this stitch over the second stitch and off the right needle.

3. One stitch remains on the right needle as shown. Knit the next stitch. Repeat from the * (in step 1) until you have bound off the required number of stitches. ■

In some patterns, you are instructed to bind off purlwise, either because the right side of the work is the purl side, or because the design calls for the bind-off to be on the wrong side.

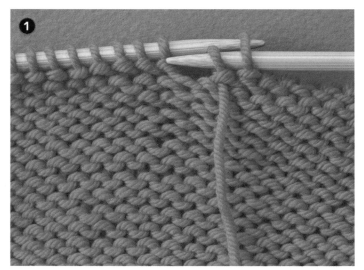

1. Knit two stitches. *Insert the left needle from behind into the first stitch (the one further from the tip) on the right needle.

2. Pull this stitch over the second stitch and off the right needle.

3. One stitch remains on the right needle as shown. Purl the next stitch. Repeat from the * (in step 1) until you have bound off the required number of stitches. ∎

You can join two pieces of knitting together and bind off at the same time. This method is commonly used for shoulder seams, but also for other items as well. It provides an almost seamless appearance when worked as shown below. But, when worked with the wrong sides facing, it forms a decorative ridge.

1. Hold the two needles so that the points are facing the same direction and the wrong (purl) side of each piece is on the outside.

2. Bring the needles together (the right side of the two pieces facing each other on the inside). Insert an empty third needle knitwise into the first stitch of each needle.

3. Wrap the yarn around the right (inserted) needle as if to knit, as shown, then knit these two stitches together and drop them from the left needles. *Knit the next two stitches together as before.

4. There are now two stitches on the third needle. Pass the first stitch over the second stitch as in the regular knit bind-off. Repeat from the * (in step 3) until you have bound off the required number of stitches. ■

Joining Yarn

Soon enough, you will be knitting along and realize that your yarn ball is looking smaller and smaller. It's time to join yarn.

Joining yarn works best at the end of a row. That way, it will be easier to weave in your ends without creating too much of a bulge. Simply tie the new yarn loosely around the old yarn, leaving at least a 6" (15cm) tail. When your project is finished, untie the knot and weave in the ends.

To change yarn in the middle of a row, simply poke your right needle into the next stitch, but wrap the new yarn around the needle in place of the old yarn and keep on knitting. After you've reached the end of a row, tie the old and new strands together so that they don't unravel.

Weaving In Ends

At the end of a project, you'll have loose ends. In order to hide those strands and create a product that truly looks finished, you must weave the loose ends into the wrong side of the knitted fabric.

To begin, carefully untie the knot you made when first joining new yarn. Then take a loose strand and thread it through the yarn needle, snaking the needle (and attached yarn) up and down through approximately five loops near the edge of your knitting. Remember to snip close to the work to remove whatever's left, but be careful not to cut into the actual knitting. Then thread the second strand through the needle and weave up.

If you have changed the yarn in the middle of a row, untie the knot and weave one loose piece in each direction horizontally, following the path of the affected stitch through five or six additional stitches on the wrong side of the work. You should always double-check the right side of the fabric to make sure no puckering or slackness has occurred.

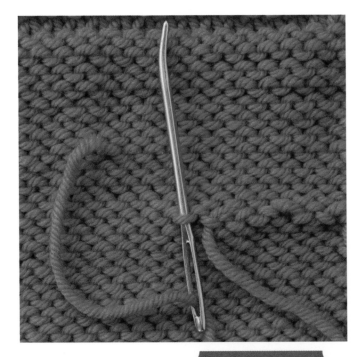

GOOD TO KNOW

TIP Always double-check the right side of the fabric to make sure no puckering or slackness has occurred.

Beyond Knitting & Purling

Moving Ahead with Techniques

There's more to knitting than the basic knit and purl stitches. Once you've used them to create scarves to your heart's content and blankets for all the babies among your friends and family, it's time to advance to go further. The techniques of shaping, ribbing, reading schematics, and getting the right stitch gauge are simple, and learning them will open you up to new knitting horizons. Once you learn these next steps, you're almost ready for the exciting world of sweater making!

Checking Your Gauge

Knitting gauge—the number of rows and stitches per inch—determines the size of the garment (or bag, or blanket) you are making. It's also one of the most important factors in your knitting. Every pattern states the gauge on which the sizing for the project is based. If you don't get it right, you risk ending up with a garment that doesn't fit. And since everything from the size and brand of the needles you're using to how loosely or tightly you knit can affect your gauge, you should always, always, always test your knitting against the pattern gauge before you begin the project. How do you do this? Simple.

You make a gauge swatch.

The gauge swatch is the first step in garment making. This is a square piece of knitted fabric that demonstrates how you, the needles, and the yarn interact before you get going on the main project. You will find a recommended gauge, or stitches and rows per inch, at the beginning of the instructions on every project, usually directly beneath the suggestions for yarn weight and needle size.

To create the gauge swatch, gather the exact yarn and needles you plan to use for your project. Even the smallest differences such as yarn color and needle brand can affect your gauge. Cast on enough stitches to create a square at least 4 inches wide—anywhere from 12-20 depending upon the size of the needles and the thickness of the yarn you are using should do it. You can use the number of stitches recommended in the pattern gauge as a guide. Then knit or work in the specified stitch pattern until the square is a little more than four inches high.

Slip the stitches off the needle, bind off, and put the swatch down on a table or other smooth, hard surface.

1. Use a tape measure or ruler to measure four inches across the swatch. Shown here is the tape measure over the stitches between the garter selvage stitches. Count the number of stitches in those four inches. Compare this number to the stitches given in the stated gauge.

2. Using the same ruler or tape, measure from the bottom to the top of the swatch. Shown here is the tape measure over the rows between the garter stitch rows. Count the number of rows in those four inches. Compare this number to the rows given in the stated gauge.

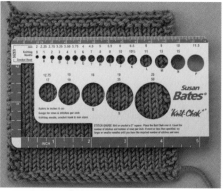

3. You can also use a stitch gauge to get the same results. Place the gauge on your swatch and count the stitches across horizontally and the rows vertically, that appear in the window.

WHAT IS A STITCH GAUGE?

A stitch gauge is a flat rectangle of metal or plastic that simplifies the process of measuring gauge by providing a little window through which you can easily count stitches. First, lay your knitting down on a flat surface and then line up the L-shaped window with the corner of a stitch. Count the number of Vs in the window (both horizontally and vertically) to get accurate stitch and row gauges.

Another feature of stitch gauges is a row of holes that can be used to identify the size of unmarked needles. To do this, slip the needle into holes of increasing size until you reach a hole that lets the needle pass all the way through. The corresponding number is the needle size.

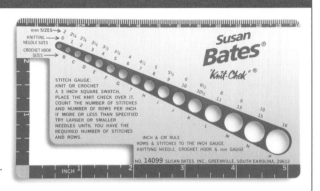

RECHECK YOUR GAUGE

When you are as near as achievable to the recommended gauge, go ahead and begin knitting your garment, but don't forget about gauge in general just yet. At times, the gauge of your actual garment may change dramatically from the gauge of your original swatch. After you've worked about five inches of your project, recheck your gauge by laying the piece down on a flat surface and pulling out your tape measure (or stitch gauge) again. Your knitting should be as near to the suggested gauge as it was before. In the event that it's not, you'll have to unravel what you've done and start again using a different needle size. As you rip out the rows and roll the yarn back into a ball,

remember it is better to do this now and have a usable garment in the long run.

ALWAYS MAKE THE GAUGE SWATCH

Knitters sometimes mistakenly believe that creating the gauge swatch is an extra, unnecessary step that can be avoided altogether. This is not true. Always make the gauge swatch. Let's say your knitting is one half stitch off of the suggested gauge—your whole garment can end up unwearable! There's nothing quite as frustrating as working diligently on a project that doesn't fit properly.

Both swatches shown here have exactly the same number of stitches and rows, but the one on the left **(1)** was stitched with larger needles than the one on the right

(2). As you can see, the row gauge is as important to a good fit as the stitch gauge. Always knit a gauge swatch for every project, without exception.

You can make the gauge swatch easier to work with by including selvage stitches on the edges of the square. Selvage stitches help the piece of fabric lay nice and flat, as well as making measuring easier, by giving you clear-cut edges between which to measure. To craft selvage stitches, work two rows of garter stitch (knit every row) at the top and bottom of the swatch and include two stitches in garter stitch at the beginning and end of each stockinette row.

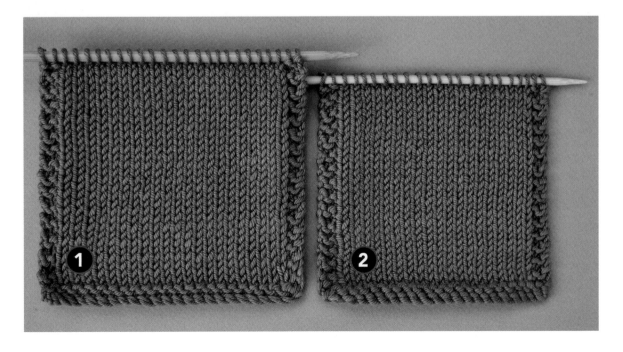

Knitting Abbreviations and Terms

These letters, numbers, and symbols are part of a system of knitting terminology that saves space in patterns. Here, we list and describe the terms you'll run across in this book.

approx approximately

beg begin, beginning

ch 1 chain one (crochet loop)

cont continue

cn cable needle

dec decrease

dpn double-pointed needle(s)

in/cm/mm inches/centimeters/millimeters

inc increase

inc (dec)...sts evenly across row
Count the number of stitches in the row, and then divide that number by the number of stitches to be increased (decreased). The result of this division will tell you how many stitches to work between each increased (decreased) stitch.

k knit

k the knit and p the purl sts
This is a phrase used when a pattern of knit and purl stitches has been established and will be continued for some time. When the stitch that's facing you looks like a V, knit it. When it looks like a bump, purl it.

k2tog Knit two stitches together to decrease one stitch.

k3tog Knit three stitches together. (Worked same as a k2tog, but insert needle into three stitches instead of two for a double decrease.)

kfb Knit in front and back of next stitch to increase one stitch. (Also called bar increase.)

knitwise Insert the needle into the stitch as if you were going to knit it.

LH left hand

M1 make one
With the needle tip, lift the strand between the last stitch knit and the next stitch on the left-hand needle and knit into the back of it. One knit stitch has been added.

oz/g ounces/grams (usually in reference to amount of yarn in a single ball)

p purl

p2tog Purl two stitches together to decrease one stitch.

pat pattern

pm place marker

purlwise Insert the needle into the stitch as if you were going to purl it.

rem remain, remains, or remaining

rep repeat

rep from * Repeat the instructions after the asterisk as many times as indicated. If the directions say "rep from * to end," continue to repeat the instructions after the asterisk to the end of the row.

reverse shaping A term used for garments like cardigans where shaping for the right and left fronts is identical, but reversed. For example, neck edge stitches decreased at the beginning of the row for the first piece will be decreased at the end of the row on the second. In general, follow the directions for the first piece, being sure to mirror the decreases or increases on each side.

RH right hand

RS right side

sc single crochet

SKP Slip one stitch knitwise to right-hand needle. Knit the next stitch and pass the slipped stitch over the knit stitch to decrease one stitch.

SK2P Slip one stitch, knit two stitches together, pass slipped stitch over the two stitches knit together to decrease two stitches.

sl st slip a stitch

slip Transfer the indicated stitches from the left to the right needle without working (knitting or purling) them.

Small (Medium, Large) The most common method of displaying changes in pattern for different sizes. In general, the measurements, stitch counts, directions, etc. for the smallest size come first, followed by the increasingly larger sizes in parentheses. When there is only one number given, it applies to all of the sizes.

ssk Slip two stitches knitwise one at a time and knit them together through the back loop to decrease one stitch.

St st stockinette stitch

st/sts stitch/stitches

tbl through the back loop

tog together

work even Continue in the established pattern without working any increases or decreases.

WS wrong side

wyib with yarn in back

wyif with yarn in front

yo yarn over

Understanding Schematics

When you reach the end of most sweater patterns, you will find line drawings with bullets and numbers skirting the sides, and words like "Back" and "Left Front" across the centers. These are called schematics, and have some very important uses in our task at hand.

The first thing to remember is that schematics are drawn to scale. They give you an at-a-glance rundown of all the measurements, angles, and shapes of the sweater you're making. Schematics will also reveal if the sweater tapers at the waist or narrows at the shoulders, and indicate the exact depth and width of the armholes, bust, and sleeves. Schematics provide

you with an idea of what your sweater pieces will look like when completed. When blocking the pieces of a garment, schematics will be very useful.

In general, the simpler the sweater the simpler the schematic. The drawings on this page are good examples of schematics for a beginner-level woman's pullover sweater. The numbers preceding the parentheses represent the smallest size, while the numbers inside the parentheses indicate measurements for sequentially increasing sizes. For cardigans, one of the two front pieces will be drawn, and then you just have to visualize (or sketch) a mirror image for the other.

A SAMPLE SCHEMATIC

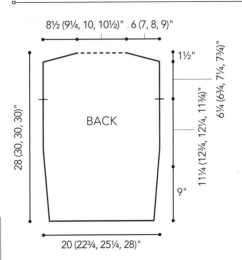

8½ (9¼, 10, 10½)" 6 (7, 8, 9)"

BACK

28 (30, 30, 30)"

1½"

6¼ (6¾, 7¼, 7¾)"

11¼ (12¾, 12¼, 11¾)"

9"

20 (22¾, 25¼, 28)"

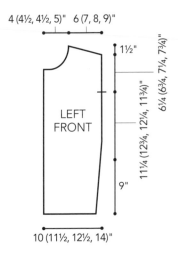

4 (4½, 4½, 5)" 6 (7, 8, 9)"

LEFT FRONT

1½"

6¼ (6¾, 7¼, 7¾)"

11¼ (12¾, 12¼, 11¾)"

9"

10 (11½, 12½, 14)"

The schematic drawing on the left shows the left front and back piece of a cardigan. The numbers along the sides indicate the measurement of each section between the dots.

The schematic on the right shows the sleeve piece of the cardigan.

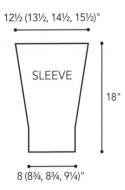

12½ (13½, 14½, 15½)"

SLEEVE

18"

8 (8¾, 8¾, 9¼)"

Decreasing

Decreasing (or reducing the number of stitches in a row) is a method of creating shaping within a knitted piece. Two of the easiest and most common decreases are the knit two together (or k2tog) and purl two together (or p2tog) decreases.

K2TOG: Insert the right needle from front to back (knitwise) into the next two stitches on the left needle. Wrap the yarn around the right needle (as when knitting). Draw the yarn through both stitches on the left needle and pull it through, then drop the stitches from the needle. There is one new knit stitch on the right needle. You have decreased one stitch.

K2TOG TBL: Insert the right needle from behind the left needle and into the next two stitches on the left needle, as shown. Draw the yarn through both stitches on the left needle and pull it through, then drop the stitches from the needle. There is one new knit stitch on the right needle. You have decreased one stitch.

P2TOG: Insert the right needle into the front loops (purlwise) of the next two stitches on the left needle. Wrap the yarn around the right needle (as when purling) and pull it through. There is one new purl stitch on the right needle. You have decreased one stitch.

Increasing

Increasing also changes the number of stitches, and there are various ways to do it. The bar increase is one of the most common.

BAR INCREASE (KFB)

1. To increase on the knit side, insert the right needle knitwise into the stitch to be increased. Wrap the yarn around the right needle and pull it through as if knitting, but leave the stitch on the left needle.

2. Insert the right needle into the back of the same stitch. Wrap the yarn around the needle and pull it through. Slip the stitch off the left needle. You now have two new stitches on the right needle and have increased one stitch. ■

Techniques to Know

Here are a few commonly used techniques.

WORKING INTO FRONT AND BACK LOOPS

The loop closest to you is the front of the stitch. This is the loop you'll normally work into. To knit into the front loop, insert the right needle from left to right into the stitch on the left needle. To purl into the front loop, insert needle from right to left into the stitch.

To knit into the back loop (loop farthest from you), insert the right needle from right to left under the left needle and into the stitch. To purl into the back loop, insert the needle from behind into the stitch.

Knitting into the back loop

Purling into the back loop

KNITTING OR PURLING IN THE ROW BELOW

Some pattern stitches require you to knit and purl in the same row or even to work into the row below to create an elongated stitch.

K1b: With yarn at back of the work, insert right needle from front to back into the center of the stitch one row below the next stitch on the left needle and knit this stitch. Slip the top stitch off the left needle.

P1b: With yarn at front of the work, insert right needle from back to front into the center of the stitch one row below the next stitch on the left needle and purl this stitch. Slip the top stitch off the left needle.

WITH YARN IN FRONT AND BACK

When switching from knit to purl stitches, or vice versa, you must have the yarn in the correct position to work the next stitch. Before working a knit stitch, the yarn must be at the back; before a purl stitch, the yarn must be at the front. Always move the yarn *between* the needles when changing its position unless the pattern states otherwise.

With yarn in back **(WYIB)**

With yarn in front **(WYIF)**

Knitting in the Round

Instead of working back and forth as you do with straight needles, you simply keep knitting (or purling) in a spiral, creating a tube rather than a flat piece of knitting. To do this, you are going to need circular or double point needles.

HOW TO USE CIRCULAR NEEDLES

Circular needles can be found in several lengths. You'll need to choose one that is long enough to hold all of your stitches but

short enough so the stitches are not stretched when joined. Your pattern instructions will tell you how long the needles need to be. Cast on your stitches just as you would for straight knitting, taking care not to twist the stitches. (If you do, your fabric will end up twisted, too.) The last stitch you cast on will be the last stitch in your round. Place a marker over the needle so you'll know where the round ends, then follow the instructions shown below.

1. Hold the needle tip with the last cast-on stitch in your right hand and the tip with the first cast-on stitch in your left hand. Knit the first cast-on stitch, pulling the yarn tight to avoid a gap.

2. Work until you reach the marker. This completes the first round. Slip the marker to the right needle and work the next round. Shown here are three stitches that have been worked in the next round after slipping the marker. As you join rounds, make sure the stitches are not twisted. Keeping the cast-on edge facing the center will help keep things straight. ∎

GOOD TO KNOW

FLAT KNITTING WITH CIRCULAR NEEDLES

Circular needles can also be used for "flat" knitting. You simply flip the work over at the end of a row and continue stitching as you would with straight needles.

Double-pointed needles can also be used for knitting in the round. The process is the same as for circular needles, but with stitches divided evenly among three or four double pointed needles. This method is ideal for knitting socks, hats, or any tube shape that decreases to a smaller point.

Distribute the cast-on stitches among two to three double-pointed needles by sliding them from the end of the original needle to which they were cast on. Being careful not to twist your work, with an empty fourth (or fifth) needle, knit the first cast-on stitch and continue to the end of the first needle; *with the empty needle, knit the stitches from the next needle; repeat from the * to the end of the round. Be sure to pull the working yarn tight from needle to needle to avoid any gaps in your work. Place a marker to mark the first needle and the beginning of the round.

You will make a mistake from time to time—we all do. However, as long as you know how to fix those mistakes, it's no big deal. Here is how to fix the most common mistakes.

PICKING UP A DROPPED KNIT STITCH

Knit Side

1. This method is used when a knit stitch has been dropped only one row. Work to where the stitch was dropped. Be sure that the loose strand is behind the dropped stitch.

2. Insert the right needle from front to back into the dropped stitch and under the loose horizontal strand behind.

3. Insert the left needle from the back into the dropped stitch on the right needle, and pull this stitch over the loose strand as shown. Transfer this newly made stitch back to the left needle by inserting the left needle from front to back into the stitch and slipping it off the right needle. ■

PICKING UP A DROPPED PURL STITCH

Purl Side

1. This method is used when a purl stitch has been dropped only one row. Work to the dropped purl stitch. Be sure that the loose horizontal strand is in front of the dropped stitch.

2. Insert the right needle from back to front into the dropped stitch, and then under the loose horizontal strand. With the left needle, lift the dropped stitch over the horizontal strand and off the right needle. Transfer the newly made purl stitch back to the left needle by inserting the left needle from front to back into the stitch and slipping it off the right needle. ■

GOOD TO KNOW

CROCHET CHAIN

Knowing how to make a crochet chain is a very useful skill. It can be used for a button loop, a tie at the top of a hat, or even a skinny belt.

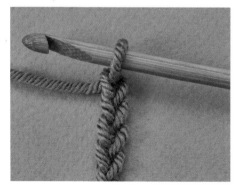

1. Make a slip knot and place the loop on a crochet hook. With the hook in your right hand and yarn in your left hand, *wrap the yarn around the hook as shown.

2. Bring the yarn through the loop on the hook to make one chain. Repeat from the * in step one to the desired number of chain. Cut the yarn and draw the end through the last loop to fasten off. ■

Knit Side

If you accidentally bring the yarn back over the top of the needle at the beginning of the knit row, the first stitch will have two loops instead of one, as shown.

To avoid creating this extra stitch, keep the yarn under the needle when taking it to the back to knit the first stitch of a new row. ■

Purl Side

At the beginning of a purl row, if the yarn is at the back, and then brought to the front under the needle, the first stitch will have two loops instead of one, as shown.

To avoid making these two loops, the yarn should be at the front before you purl the first stitch. ■

A Basic Stitch Sampler

Using Stitches for Interest

Once you've grown confident with the basics, you'll want to go further. There are two ways to add interest to knitted fabrics—color and texture. At this point, you can add colorwork and stitch patterns to the equation for a beautiful outcome. This is when your project becomes a lot more interesting. This chapter provides a variety of textured stitch patterns for you to try.

Alternating whole rows of knit and purl stitches creates the popular stockinette stitch. However, knit and purl stitches can be combined in many different ways to create all kinds of interesting textural patterns. To do this, switch back and forth between knit and purl stitches within the same row.

RIBBING

BASIC TEXTURES

RAISED STITCHES

LACE

BASIC CABLES

Ribbing

Ribbing is the most popular knit/purl stitch. It is stretchy and has the ability to "bounce" back into place, making ribbing ideal for hems, necks, and cuffs of most sweaters. With ribbing, you can also make a complete garment.

Ribbing is easy to do. In the most basic form, you knit one stitch, purl the next, and keep alternating until you reach the end of the row. Once you've done a row or two, you can put down your instructions and let the stitches show you what to do. Knit the stitches that look like a "V" and purl the ones that look like a bump. Most popular among ribbings are k1, p1 and k2, p2 combinations, seen on many sweaters. But you can knit a ribbing in just about any combination of knits and purls.

TWISTED K1, P1 (HALF TWIST)

(over an odd number of sts)

Row 1 (right side) K1 through the back loop, *p1, k1 through the back loop; rep from * to end.
Row 2 P1, *k1, p1 rep from * to end.

Rep rows 1 and 2. ∎

TWISTED K1, P1 (FULL TWIST)

(over an odd number of sts)

Row 1 (right side) K1 through the back loop, *p1, k1 through the back loop; rep from * to end.
Row 2 P1 through the back loop, *k1, p1 through the back loop; rep from * to end.

Rep rows 1 and 2. ∎

K5, P2

(multiple of 7 sts plus 2)

Row 1 (right side) P2, *k5, p2; rep from * to end.
Row 2 K2, *p5, k2; rep from * to end.

Rep rows 1 and 2. ∎

K2, P5
(multiple of 7 sts plus 2)

Row 1 (right side) K2, *p5, k2;
rep from * to end.
Row 2 P2, *k5, p2; rep from * to end.

Rep rows 1 and 2. ■

Basic Textures

You'll be pleasantly surprised to discover that some of the prettiest textured stitches are the easiest to knit. The seed stitch, for example, requires a simple knit one, purl one, and alternates on the next row with purl one, knit one.

SEED STITCH
(over an even number of sts)

Row 1 (RS) *K1, p1; rep from * to end.
Row 2 *P1, k1; rep from * to end.

Rep rows 1 and 2. ■

SAND STITCH

(multiple of 2 sts plus 1)

Row 1 (RS) K1, *p1; k1;
rep from * to end.
Row 2 Purl.
Row 3 P1, *k1, p1; rep from * to end.
Row 4 Purl.

Rep rows 1–4. ∎

HORIZONTAL DASH STITCH

(multiple of 10 sts plus 6)

Row 1 (RS) P6, *k4, p6;
rep from * to end.
Row 2 and all WS rows Purl.
Row 3 Knit.
Row 5 P1, *k4, p6; rep from *,
end last rep p1.
Row 7 Knit.
Row 8 Purl.

Rep rows 1–8. ∎

BASKETWEAVE

(multiple of 8 sts plus 5)

Row 1 (RS) Knit.
Row 2 K5, *p3, k5; rep from * to end.
Row 3 P5, *k3, p5; rep from * to end.
Row 4 Rep row 2.
Row 5 Knit.
Row 6 K1, *p3, k5; rep from *,
end last rep k1.
Row 7 P1, *k3, p5; rep from *,
end last rep p1.
Row 8 Rep row 6.

Rep rows 1–8. ∎

EMBOSSED DIAMONDS

(multiple of 10 sts plus 3)

Row 1 (RS) P1, k1, p1, *[k3, p1] twice, k1, p1; rep from * to end.
Row 2 P1, k1, *p3, k1, p1, k1, p3, k1; rep from *, end p1.
Row 3 K4, *[p1, k1] twice, p1, k5; rep from * to last 4 sts, k4.
Row 4 P3, *[k1, p1] 3 times, k1, p3; rep from * to end.
Row 5 Rep row 3.

Row 6 Rep row 2.
Row 7 Rep row 1.
Row 8 P1, k1, p1, *k1, p5, [k1, p1] twice; rep from * to end.
Row 9 [P1, k1] twice, *p1, k3, [p1, k1] 3 times; rep from * to last 9 sts, p1, k3, [p1, k1] twice, p1.
Row 10 Rep row 8.

Rep rows 1–10. ■

Raised Stitches

Raised stitches such as knots and popcorns are a great way to add texture to garments. When knitting a raised stitch, you'll be increasing several stitches in one stitch and knitting a little ball that sticks up on the surface of your knitting. Knots are made by forming little loops on the front of the knitting. Raised stitches can be placed randomly or in a regular pattern to create overall texture.

PEPPERCORN STITCH

(multiple of 4 sts plus 3)

Peppercorn st Knit next st, [sl st just knit back to LH needle and knit it again tbl] 3 times.
Row 1 (RS) K3, *peppercorn st, k3; rep from * to end.
Row 2 Purl.
Row 3 K1, *peppercorn st, k3; rep from *, end last rep k1.
Row 4 Purl.

Rep rows 1–4. ■

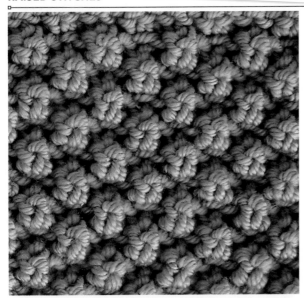

TRINITY STITCH

(multiple of 4 sts)

Row 1 (RS) Purl.
Row 2 *[K1, p1, k1] in same st, p3tog; rep from * to end.
Row 3 Purl.
Row 4 *P3tog, [k1, p1, k1] in same st; rep from * to end.

Rep rows 1–4. ■

DOT-KNOT STITCH

(multiple of 5 sts plus 1)

Dot-Knot Stitch Insert RH needle from front to back under horizontal strand between 1st and 2nd sts on LH needle, wrap yarn and draw through a loop loosely; insert RH needle between same sts above horizontal strand, draw through another loop loosely; bring yarn to front between needles and purl the first st on LH needle with point of LH needle, pass the first loop over the 2nd loop and the purled st and off needle; pass the 2nd loop over the purled st and off needle.

Row 1 (RS) Knit.
Row 2 and all WS rows Purl.
Row 3 K3, *work dot-knot stitch, k5; rep from *, end last rep k3.
Row 5 Knit
Row 7 *Work dot-knot st, k5; rep from *, end k1.
Row 8 Purl.

Rep rows 1–8. ■

Lace

It's easy to learn how to knit simple eyelet trims and inserts once you learn to make a yarn over (yo). A yarn over creates a hole in the fabric. After a knit stitch, bring the yarn to the front between the needles, then bring it over the needle from front to back to work the next stitch.

EYELET ROWS

(multiple of 2 sts plus 2)

Rows 1, 5, 7, 9, 13, and 15 (RS) Knit.
Row 2 and all WS rows Purl.
Row 3 K1, *yo, SKP; rep from *, end k1.
Row 11 K1, *SKP, yo; rep from *, end k1
Row 16 Knit.

Rep rows 1–16. ■

CHEVRON EYELETS

(multiple of 9 sts)

Row 1 (RS) *K4, yo, SKP, k3; rep from * to end.
Row 2 and all WS rows Purl.
Row 3 *K2, k2tog, yo, k1, yo, SKP, k2; rep from * to end.
Row 5 *K1, k2tog, yo, k3, yo, SKP, k1; rep from * to end.
Row 7 *K2tog, yo, k5, yo, SKP; rep from * to end.
Row 8 Purl.

Rep rows 1–8. ■

CHEVRON LACE
(multiple of 8 sts plus 1)

Row 1 (RS) K1, *yo, k2, SK2P, k2, yo, k1; rep from * to end.
Row 2 Purl.

Rep rows 1 and 2. ■

OPENWORK LEAF
(multiple of 8 sts plus 1)

Row 1 (RS) K1, *yo, k2, S2KP, k2, yo, k1; rep from * to end.
Row 2 and all WS rows Purl.
Row 3 K1, *k1, yo, k1, SK2P, k1, yo, k2; rep from * to end.
Row 5 K1, * k2, yo, SK2P, yo, k3; rep from * to end.
Row 7 K2tog, *k2, yo, k1, yo, k2, SK2P; rep from * to last 2 sts, end SKP.

Row 9 K2tog, *k1, yo, k3, yo, k1, SK2P; rep from * to last 2 sts, end SKP.
Row 11 K2tog, *yo, k5, yo, SK2P; rep from * to last 2 sts, end SKP.
Row 12 Purl.

Rep rows 1–12. ■

Basic Cables

To make cables, you will need a small, double-pointed needle called a cable needle (cn). By knitting your stitches "out of order," you create a twisted effect. Simply slip the stitches to be worked last to the cable needle and hold to the back or front as directed. Work the next stitches on the left needle, then work the held stitches and continue to work the rest of the row.

MOCK CABLE

(multiple of 4 sts plus 2)

2-st right twist (RT) K2tog leaving both sts on needle; insert RH needle between 2 sts, and knit first st again; then sl both sts from needle.

Row 1 (RS) P2, *k2 , p2; rep from * to end.
Row 2 and 4 K2, *p2, k2; rep from * to end.
Row 3 P2, *RT, p2; rep from * to end.

Rep rows 1–4. ■

GIANT RIGHT CABLE

(panel of 16 sts)

12-st right cable Sl 6 sts to cn and hold to *back* of work, k6, k6 from cn.

Row 1 and 3 (RS) P2, k12, p2.
Row 2 and all WS rows K the knit sts and p the purl sts.
Row 5 P2, 12-st right cable, p2.
Row 7 Rep row 1.
Row 8 Rep row 2.

Rep rows 1–8. ■

GIANT LEFT CABLE

(panel of 16 sts)

12-st left cable Sl 6 sts to cn and hold to *front* of work, k6, k6 from cn.

Row 1 and 3 (RS) P2, k12, p2.
Row 2 and all WS rows K the knit sts and p the purl sts.
Row 5 P2, 12-st left cable, p2.
Row 7 Rep row 1.
Row 8 Rep row 2.

Rep rows 1–8. ■

Finishing

Final Touches

Finishing involves only a few simple steps: blocking (shaping the pieces you've knit), sewing those pieces together, and weaving in all the loose ends. We'll also show you some other finishing touches, such as how to make buttonholes.

Finishing Your Work with Blocking

Sometimes, the freshly knit garment may appear wavy and misshapen. This is where blocking comes in. Blocking is the process of pinning a knitted piece to a blocking board, then lightly wetting the yarn and allowing it to dry. Yarn is very forgiving; it will hold whatever shape it's been pinned down in once it dries. Without blocking, even a perfectly knit garment wouldn't look right.

Wet and steam are the two main methods of blocking. The Pressing Guide on this page will help you determine which is best for your project. But before beginning either method, gather up any schematics or measurements from the pattern. Then you will know the exact shape to pin the pieces.

WHAT YOU'LL NEED

1. Flat, covered, padded surface large enough to hold one piece of knitting (for example, carpet or bed covered with plastic and a towel)
2. Rust-proof T-pins (NOT pins with little plastic colored heads—these will melt during steam blocking, creating a huge mess)
3. Tape measure
4. Spray bottle with cool water (or basin full of cool water) or steam iron (or handheld steamer)
5. Towels (be sure they're colorfast)
6. Pressing cloth

WET BLOCKING

For wet blocking, immerse the knitted pieces in cool water, squeeze them out, and stretch them on a flat surface to their exact measurements according to the schematics. Or you can pin the pieces first and then wet them down with a water-filled spray bottle. Your personal preference will determine the method you use, though you may find the spraying method to be less awkward. Once the pieces are wet, leave them there until they are completely dry. This may take twenty-four hours or more, so be patient.

STEAM BLOCKING

For steam blocking, first pin the pieces on a flat surface according to the schematics. Fire up your steam iron or handheld steamer, and when it's ready, hold the iron close to the fabric until the fabric is convincingly damp. Never touch the iron to the stitches! If you must press lightly, protect your knitted piece by sandwiching a colorfast towel or pressing cloth between the fabric and the hot metal. As with wet blocking, leave the pieces to dry completely. Drying time after steaming probably won't take as long as it does for wet blocking, but you may still need to wait for several hours.

PRESSING GUIDE

Fibers will react differently to heat, so it is best to know what to expect before you press or steam them. Remember that there are many combinations of fibers. You should choose the process that is suited to all the components of the garment. If you are unsure about the fiber content of your yarn, test your gauge swatch before blocking your sweater pieces.

Angora Wet block by spraying.

Cotton Wet block or warm/hot steam press.

Linen Wet block or warm/hot steam press.

Lurex Do not block.

Mohair Wet block by spraying.

Novelties Do not block.

Synthetics Carefully follow instructions on ball band—usually wet block by spraying. Do not press.

Wool and all wool-like fibers (alpaca, camel hair, cashmere) Wet block by spraying or warm steam press.

Wool blends Wet block by spraying; do not press unless tested.

Joining Your Work with Seams

There's one thing left to do to make your pieces wearable: Sew them together. Sewing together, or "seaming," is achieved with a yarn needle and the same yarn used to make your project.

Sewing together knitted fabric can be done in many different ways, with each method serving a different purpose. One kind of seaming is best for joining adjacent lengths of stockinette stitch, and another is better for connecting vertical and horizontal pieces of the same fabric.

Pattern instructions sometimes recommend a particular method to use. Make sure you have correctly lined up your stitches before sewing the seams. Find the cast-on stitches on both sides. Pin the stitches together with a straight pin or safety pin. Count up ten rows on each side and pin the corresponding stitches together. Continue until you get to the top of the two pieces. When creating a garment like a hat, the rows should line up exactly. If you end up with extra rows on one side, go back and see where stragglers might have occurred on the opposite side. If you are seaming two pieces, you may have to ease in extra rows if one piece is slightly longer than the other. Note that a contrasting color yarn is used in the photos for clarity. Use the same color yarn when seaming.

HOW TO BEGIN SEAMING

If there is a long tail left from your cast-on row, you can use this strand to begin sewing. To make a neat join at the lower edge with no gap, use the technique shown here.

Thread the strand into a yarn needle. With the right sides of both pieces facing you, insert the needle from back to front into the corner stitch of the piece without the tail. Making a figure 8 with the yarn, insert the needle from back to front into the stitch with the cast-on tail. Tighten to close the gap.

VERTICAL SEAM ON STOCKINETTE STITCH

The vertical seam is worked from the right side and is used to join two edges row by row. It hides the uneven stitches at the edge of a row and creates an invisible seam, making the knitting appear continuous.

Insert the yarn needle under the horizontal bar between the first and second stitches. Insert the needle into the corresponding bar on the other piece. Continue alternating from side to side.

VERTICAL SEAM ON GARTER STITCH

This seam joins two edges row by row like vertical seaming on stockinette stitch. The alternating pattern of catching top and bottom stitch loops makes the join nearly invisible.

Insert the yarn needle into the top loop on one side, then in the bottom loop of the corresponding stitch on the other side. Continue to alternate in this way.

HORIZONTAL SEAM ON STOCKINETTE STITCH

This seam is used to join two bound-off edges, such as for shoulder seams or hoods, and is worked stitch by stitch. You must have the same number of stitches on each piece so that the finished seam will resemble a continuous row of knit stitches. Be sure to pull the yarn tight enough to hide the bound-off edges.

With the bound-off edges together, lined up stitch for stitch, insert the yarn needle under a stitch inside the bound-off edge of one side and then under the corresponding stitch on the other side. Repeat all the way across the join.

Used to connect a bound-off edge to a vertical length of knitted fabric, this seam requires careful pre-measuring and marking to ensure an even seam.

Insert the needle under one or two horizontal bars between the first and second stitches of the horizontal piece, shown here. Then insert the needle under a stitch inside the bound-off edge on the vertical piece. Alternate in this way.

Picking Up Stitches

Sometimes you will need to "pick up stitches." One picks up stitches with a knitting needle or crochet hook and a new strand of yarn, dipping into and out of the edge of the knitted fabric, creating new loops. These new loops will serve as the foundation for a collar, button band, sleeve, baby bootie instep, etc.

For picking up stitches along a straight edge, focus on the two S's: side and spacing. For the first "S," be sure to pick up stitches with the right side facing out. The second "s" reminds you to space the stitches evenly along the fabric. Make sure that the loops you pick up aren't clustered together or separated by vast expanses along the knitted edge.

PICKING UP AT THE NECK
When picking up stitches for a sloped edge (such as for a neck), take a little more care than for a straight edge. Much of this effort comes in the spacing. It's especially important that the stitches be picked up evenly when you are making a neckband, so the band will not flare out (too many stitches picked up) or pull in (too few stitches picked up).

PICKING UP ALONG A BOUND-OFF OR SIDE EDGE

1. Insert the knitting needle into the corner stitch of the first row, one stitch in from the side edge. Wrap the yarn around the needle knitwise. Draw the yarn through. You have picked up one stitch. Continue to pick up stitches along the edge.

2. When picking up along a side edge, insert the needle from front to back one stitch in from the edge. Wrap yarn around the needle and draw it through to make one stitch. Continue to pick up stitches. Occasionally skip one row to keep the edge from flaring.

We will study the two-row horizontal buttonhole, the one-row horizontal buttonhole, and the yarn-over buttonhole. The two-row and one-row buttonholes are shown worked over four stitches, though you might want to use more or less depending on the size of your button.

TWO-ROW HORIZONTAL BUTTONHOLE

The most common buttonhole is undoubtedly the two-row horizontal buttonhole. Make it by binding off a number of stitches on one row and casting them on again on the next. The last stitch bound off is part of the left side of the buttonhole.

1. On the first row, work to the placement of the buttonhole. Knit two, with the left needle, pull one stitch over the other stitch, *knit one, pull the second stitch over the knit one; repeat from the * twice more. Four stitches have been bound off.

2. On the next row, work to the bound-off stitches and cast on four stitches as follows: Wrap the yarn around your thumb to make a loop, as shown. Insert needle into loop, drop thumb and tighten on the needle.

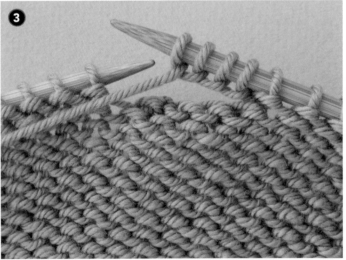

3. On the next row, work the cast-on stitches and work each stitch through the back loop to tighten them. ■

The one-row horizontal buttonhole is the neatest buttonhole and requires no further reinforcing. Although it's slightly more complicated than the two-row horizontal buttonhole, the extra effort produces a clean result.

1. Work to the buttonhole, bring yarn to front, and slip a stitch purlwise. Place yarn at back and leave it there. *Slip next stitch from left needle. Pass the first slipped stitch over it; repeat from the * three times more (not moving the yarn). Slip the last bound-off stitch to the left needle and turn work.

2. Using the knit-on cast-on, with the yarn at the back, cast on five stitches as follows: *Insert the right needle between the first and second stitches on the left needle, draw up a loop, place the loop on the left needle; repeat from the * four times more, turn the work.

3. Slip the first stitch with the yarn in back from the left needle and pass the extra cast-on stitch over it to close the buttonhole, Work to the end of the row. ■

If you are creating a smaller garment, where small buttons are more suitable, the smaller yarn-over buttonhole might be your best bet. To create this buttonhole, knit two stitches together, followed by a yarn over. On the return row, work the yarn over as a stitch.

1. After knitting two stitches together, bring the yarn from the back of the work to the front between the two needles, as shown, and knit the next stitch. There will be an extra stitch (yarn over) on the right needle.

2. On the following row, work to the yarn over, purl into the yarn over (it will be a loose stitch). The hole created by the yarn over is the buttonhole. ■

BUTTONHOLE SPACING

The goal is to space your buttonholes as evenly as possible. Accomplish this by placing markers on the button band for the first and last buttonholes. Measure the distance between them and place markers evenly for the remaining buttonholes.

Ensure your buttons and buttonholes line up in the end by following this easy tip: Count the number of rows between the lower edge and the first marker, between the first and second markers, and so on. Make a note of how many rows separate each marker, and then make your buttonholes on the corresponding rows of the buttonhole band.

ATTACHING BUTTONS

When you are ready to sew on the buttons, you can use yarn (if it will pass through the button) or matching thread. With metal buttons, which may cut the thread, you may wish to use waxed dental floss. Double the thread and tie a knot on the end. Then slip your button onto the needle and thread. You can further secure the button with a square of fabric or felt at the back, which is especially desirable on garments that receive heavy wear.

Knotted thread has a tendency to pull through knitted fabric. Lock it in place by inserting the thread into the fabric on the right side and through the doubled thread. Clip the knotted end.

GOOD TO KNOW

NOT SURE HOW MANY BUTTONS YOU NEED?
It's always best to have space for more. The smaller the gaps between buttons, the flatter and smoother your cardigan band will appear. It's also good to buy the buttons for your project before you start knitting so that you'll have an idea of the size, spacing, and number of buttonholes on the buttonhole band.

EASY BUTTONHOLE BANDS
Most patterns suggest that the button and buttonhole bands be worked separately and sewn on later. You can also work the front bands with the main piece on some styles. This easy method saves time and eliminates the need for extra seaming. This technique also allows you to space the buttonholes precisely along the edge of the sweater.

Simple Projects

It's Time to Practice Your Skills!

This collection of projects provides a chance to practice basic skills while stretching your knitting knowledge to exciting new possibilities. For further instruction on any of the techniques that follow, please visit the Pattern Help section of www.vogueknitting.com.

Skill Levels

Each skill-level section includes both accessories and garments, as well as a variety of techniques. Before deciding on a design to make, read through the instructions to see if there are techniques you have not yet tried, and practice them on the gauge swatch before beginning the project.

It is a good idea to begin with something small, such as a scarf or hat. These projects will help you to build up your skills.

●○○ Beginner	●●○ Very easy	●●● Easy
Beginner projects use basic stitches and may include simple increases, decreases, and changing colors with minimal or no finishing.	Very easy projects include simple stitch patterns and may include changing colors as well as more complex shaping and finishing.	Easy projects may include combinations of techniques or stitch patterns, changing colors, working with yarn held double, and more complex shaping and finishing.

WIDE-STRIPED COWL

PAPER BAG HAT

POMPOM WRAP

TURTLENECK PONCHO

RIBBED COWL

STRIPED MESH PULLOVER

SLEEVELESS SHELL

TURTLENECK TUNIC

GARTER CARDIGAN

HAT & COWL SET

LACE COWL

TEXTURED WRAP

SCARF & HEADBAND

SHORT-SLEEVE PULLOVER & SCARF

DROP-SHOULDER PULLOVER

CHUNKY CARDIGAN

SIMPLE PULLOVER

DOUBLE-SEED-STITCH PULLOVER

GARTER & CABLE SCARF

STRIPED HAT & SCARF

PULL-THROUGH WRAP

SLOUCHY HAT

MOHAIR CARDIGAN

CROPPED EYELET PULLOVER

BUCKET HAT

GRADIENT WRAP

PLACKET-NECKLINE PONCHO

●○○ Wide-Striped Cowl

A wide-rib rectangle with garter-stitch edges and color bands, joined at the ends to form the cowl.

KNITTED MEASUREMENTS
• Circumference 25"/65cm
• Width approx 10"/25.5cm, slightly stretched

MATERIALS
• 1 1oz/50g hank (each approx 123yd/112m) of Blue Sky Fibers *Woolstok* (fine highland wool) each in #1301 storm cloud (A), #1305 october sky (B), and #1317 midnight sea (C)

• One pair size 7 (4.5mm) needles, OR SIZE TO OBTAIN GAUGE

GAUGE
20 sts and 24 rows = 4"/10cm over St st using size 7 (4.5mm) needles. TAKE TIME TO CHECK GAUGE.

RIB PATTERN
(multiple of 12 sts plus 4)
Row 1 (RS) K2, p1, *k10, p2; rep from * to last 13 sts, k10, p1, k2.
Row 2 K3, *p10, k2; rep from * to last 13 sts, p10, k3.
Rep rows 1 and 2 for rib pat.

COWL
With A, cast on 52 sts. Work in rib pat in colors as foll: *17 rows A, 17 rows B, 17 rows C; rep from * twice more.
Piece measures approx 25"/65cm from beg. Bind off.

FINISHING
Block to measurements. Sew cast-on and bound-off edges tog to form the cowl. ■

●○○ Paper Bag Hat

The hat is worked flat with no shaping and seamed, then the crocheted tie is woven through the farrow rib fabric to close the top.

SIZES
Sized for Small, Medium, Large and shown in size Small.

KNITTED MEASUREMENTS
• Circumference approx 20 (21¼, 22½)"/51 (54, 57)cm
• Length (below tie) approx 7½ (8, 8½)"/19 (20.5, 21.5)cm

MATERIALS
• 2 (3, 3) 1¾oz/50g hanks (each approx 108yd/100m) of Tahki *Cotton Classic* (mercerized cotton) in #3783 bright teal
• One pair size 7 (4.5mm) needles OR SIZE TO OBTAIN GAUGE
• Size H/8 (5mm) crochet hook

GAUGE
21 sts and 30 rows = 4"/10cm over farrow rib using size 7 (4.5mm) needles. TAKE TIME TO CHECK GAUGE.

FARROW RIB
(over a multiple of 3 sts plus 1)
Row 1 (RS) *K2, p1; rep from *, end k1.
Row 2 P1, *k2, p1; rep from * to end.
Rep rows 1 and 2 for farrow rib.

HAT
Cast on 106 (112, 118) sts. Work in farrow rib until piece measures 9½ (10, 10½)"/ 24 (25.5, 26.5)cm from beg, end with a WS row.
Bind off in rib.

FINISHING
Sew back seam.

TIE
With crochet hook and 3 strands of yarn held tog, crochet a 24 (25, 26)"/61 (63.5, 66)cm-long chain. Fasten off, leaving a 5"/12.5cm tail for tassel. Measuring

2"/5cm down from bound-off edge, locate and mark center front of hat. Beg and ending 1"/2.5cm on either side of center front, weave chain evenly spaced through fabric 2"/5cm from bound-off edge.

TASSELS
Cut 3 strands of yarn 10"/25.5cm long. Thread strands into a large-eye yarn needle. Insert needle through tie, approx ¼"/.5cm from end. Divide strands and tail from chain evenly in half. Tie strands into a firm square knot. Trim strands to 1½"/4cm long. Rep for opposite end of tie. ∎

●○○ Pompom Wrap

Oversized wrap knit in a chunky wool yarn in twisted rib, with wide stripes and pompoms attached at the corners.

KNITTED MEASUREMENTS
- Width approx 19"/48cm
- Length 80"/204cm

MATERIALS
- 8 7.97oz/226g skeins (each approx 130yd/119m) of Brown Sheep *Burly Spun* (wool) each in #180 ruby red (A), #255 rosy velvet (B), #59 periwinkle (C) and #194 blue suede (D)
- 1 7.97oz/226g skeins (each approx 145yd/133m) of Brown Sheep *Lanaloft Sport* (wool) each in #15 roasted pepper (E) and #255 rose marquee (F)
- One pair size 13 (9mm) needles OR SIZE TO OBTAIN GAUGE

GAUGE
13 sts and 12 rows = 4"/10cm over twisted rib, unstretched, using size 13 (9mm) needles.
TAKE TIME TO CHECK GAUGE.

TWISTED RIB
Row 1 (RS) Sl 1 purlwise wyif, *k1tbl, p1tbl; rep from * to last 2 sts, k1tbl, p1.
Row 2 (WS) Sl 1 knitwise wyib, *p1tbl, k1tbl; rep from * to end.
Rep rows 1 and 2 for twisted rib.

WRAP
With A, cast on 63 sts. Work in twisted rib for 10"/25.5cm, ending with a WS row and working last k1tbl with B.
Cut A and cont in twisted rib with B for 10"/ 25.5cm, ending with a WS row and working last k1tbl with C.
Cut B and cont in twisted rib with C for 10"/ 25.5cm, ending with a WS row and working last k1tbl with D.

Cut C and cont in twisted rib with D for 20"/ 51cm, ending with a WS row and working last k1tbl with C.

Cut D and cont in twisted rib with C for 10"/ 25.5cm, ending with a WS row and working last k1tbl with B.

Cut C and cont in twisted rib with B for 10"/ 25.5cm, ending with a WS row and working last k1tbl with A.

Cut B and cont in twisted rib with A

for 10"/ 25.5cm, ending with a WS row. Bind off in pat.

POMPOMS
Make four 2"/5cm pompoms as foll: 1 with E, 1 with F and 2 with both E and F. Attach a solid or multi pompom to each corner. ∎

●○○ Turtleneck Poncho

Two rectangles are worked separately in a basketweave stitch pattern, then sewn together at the shoulder seams. The ribbed turtleneck is picked up and worked from the neck edge.

KNITTED MEASUREMENTS
- Width (flat, including ribbed edges) 35"/89cm
- Length 22"/56cm

MATERIALS
- 15 1½ oz/50g balls (each approx 120yd/110m) of Valley Yarns *Peru* (baby alpaca/merino wool) in #06 sagebrush
- One pair size 8 (5mm) needles, OR SIZE TO OBTAIN GAUGE
- Stitch holder

GAUGE
22 sts and 32 rows = 4"/10cm over basketweave st using size 8 (5mm) needles.
TAKE TIME TO CHECK GAUGE.

BASKETWEAVE STITCH
(over a multiple of 8 sts plus 2)
Row 1 (WS) P2, *k6, p2; rep from * to end.
Rows 2 and 3 K the knit sts and p the purl sts.
Row 4 Knit.
Row 5 K4, p2, *k6, p2; rep from * to last 4 sts, k4.
Rows 6 and 7 K the knit sts and p the purl sts.
Row 8 Knit.
Rep rows 1–8 for basketweave st.

BACK
Cast on 172 sts. Knit 2 rows.

BEG BASKETWEAVE ST
Row 1 (WS) P1 (selvage st), work row 1 of basketweave to last st, p1 (selvage st). Cont in pat as established, working first and last st in St st (k on RS, p on WS) for selvage sts, until piece measures 22"/56cm from beg.
Bind off.

FRONT
Work as for back until piece measures 20"/51cm from beg, end with a WS row.

NECK SHAPING
Next row (RS) Work 68 sts, place center 36 sts on a st holder, join 2nd ball of yarn and work to end. Working both sides at once, dec 1 st at each neck edge every other row 5 times—63 sts each side. Work even until same length as back. Bind off rem sts each side for shoulders.

FINISHING
Block lightly. Sew one shoulder seam.

TURTLENECK
With RS facing, pick up and k 98 sts evenly around neck edge of front and back, including sts on front neck holder.
Row 1 (WS) *P2, k2; rep from *, end p2.
Row 2 (RS) *K2, p2, rep from *, end k2.
Rep rows 1 and 2 for k2, p2 rib until turtleneck measures 9"/23cm.
Bind off loosely in rib. Sew rem shoulder and turtleneck seam.

SIDE EDGING
With RS facing, pick up and k 138 sts evenly along one side edge of front and back. Work in k2, p2 rib for 2"/5cm. Bind off loosely in rib. Work in same way along other side. ∎

●○○ Ribbed Cowl

A shoulder hugging, turtleneck cowl, worked
in the round with simple knit and purl stitches.

KNITTED MEASUREMENTS
• Shoulder circumference 40"/101.5cm
• Neck circumference
(unstretched) 21¼"/54cm
• Length (unfolded) 22½"/57cm

MATERIALS
• 7 3½ oz/100g hanks (each approx
108yd/98m) of Misti Alpaca *Hand
Paint Super Chunky* (alpaca/wool) in
#SCH07 lavender blue

• One size 13 (9mm) circular needle,
29"/74cm long
OR SIZE TO OBTAIN GAUGE

• Stitch marker

GAUGES
• 8 sts and 18 rnds = 4"/10cm over welt
pat using size 13 (9mm) needles.

• 15 sts and 12 rnds = 4"/10cm over k2,
p2 rib using size 13 (mm) needles.
TAKE TIME TO CHECK GAUGES.

WELT PATTERN
(over any number of sts)
Rnds 1–4 Purl.
Rnds 5–7 Knit.
Rep rnds 1–7 for welt pat.

K2, P2 RIB
(over a multiple of 4 sts)
Rnd 1 *K2, p2; rep from * around.
Rep rnd 1 for k2, p2 rib.

COWL
With size 13 (9mm) circular needle,
cast on 80 sts, pm and join, being careful
not to twist. Work rows 1–7 of welt pat
5 times. Knit 2 rnds. Work in k2, p2 rib until
cowl measures 22½/54cm from beg.
Bind off in rib. ■

Striped Mesh Pullover

Oversized pullover worked in a loose mesh stitch and wide stripes.

SIZES
Sized for Small/Medium, Large, X-Large/XX-Large and shown in size Small/Medium.

KNITTED MEASUREMENTS
• Bust 42 (48, 53)"/106.5 (122, 134.5)cm
• Length 22½ (24, 24)"/57 (60, 60)cm
• Upper arm 25½"/64.5cm
Note Mesh pattern is very stretchy.

MATERIALS
• 1 3½oz/100g hank (each approx 272yd/248m) of Knit One, Crochet Too *Daisy* (linen/silk/hemp) each in #209 salmon (A), #217 rose (B), #208 golden rod (C), #205 coastal blue (D), #201 snow (E) and #210 holly hock (F)

• One pair each sizes 6 and 7 (4 and 4.5mm) needles, OR SIZE TO OBTAIN GAUGE

• Stitch markers

• Stitch holders

GAUGES
• 22 sts and 22 rows = 4"/10cm over St st using smaller needles.

• 15 sts and 18 rows = 4"/10cm over mesh st using smaller needles.
TAKE TIME TO CHECK GAUGES.

NOTE
To measure as you work, make a swatch and block it. Count the number eyelets (rows) from the beginning to the measurement called for in the instructions.

3-NEEDLE BIND-OFF
1) Hold right sides of pieces together on two needles. Insert third needle knitwise into first st of each needle, and wrap yarn knitwise.
2) Knit these two sts together, and slip them off the needles. *Knit the next two sts together in the same manner.
3) Slip first st on 3rd needle over 2nd st and off needle. Rep from * in step 2 across row until all sts are bound off.

MESH PATTERN
(over an even number of sts)
Row 1 (RS) Sl 1, k1, *k2tog, yo; rep from * to last 2 sts, k2.
Row 2 Sl 1, p1, *k2tog, yo; rep from * to last 2 sts, p1, k1.
Rep rows 1 and 2 for mesh pat.

BACK
With larger needles and A, cast on 80 (90, 100) sts.
Rows 1, 3 and 5 (WS) Sl 1, p to last st, k1.
Rows 2 and 4 (RS) Sl 1, k to end.
Hem row 6 Fold work to WS, *k next st tog with corresponding st from cast-on row; rep from * to end.
Row 7 Rep row 1.
Change to smaller needles.

BEG MESH PAT
Work in mesh pat with A until piece measures 3¾ (4, 4)"/9.5 (10, 10)cm from beg, end with a WS row.
With B, work in mesh pat for 3¾ (4, 4)"/9.5 (10, 10)cm, end with a WS row.

With C, work in mesh pat for 3¾ (4, 4)"/9.5 (10, 10)cm, end with a WS row.

With D, work in mesh pat for 3¾ (4, 4)"/9.5 (10, 10)cm, end with a WS row.

With E, work in mesh pat for 3¾ (4, 4)"/9.5 (10, 10)cm, end with a WS row.

With F, work in mesh pat for 3¾ (4, 4)"/9.5 (10, 10)cm, end with a WS row.
Next row (RS) Work 20 (25, 30) sts and place on st holder, bind off 40 sts knitwise, work 20 (25, 30) sts and place on st holder.

FRONT
Work same as for back.

SLEEVES
With larger needles and E, cast on 96 sts.
Rows 1, 3 and 5 (WS) Sl 1, p to last st, k1.
Rows 2 and 4 (RS) Sl 1, k to end.
Row 6 Fold work to WS, *k next st tog with corresponding st from cast-on row; rep from * to end.
Row 7 Rep row 1.
Change to smaller needles.

BEG MESH PAT
Work in mesh pat with E until piece measures 3"/7.5cm from beg, end with a WS row.
With D, work in mesh pat for 3"/7.5cm, end with a WS row.
With A, work in mesh pat for 3"/7.5cm, end with a WS row.
Bind off.

FINISHING
Block pieces to measurements. Join shoulders using 3-needle bind-off. Place markers at front and back side edges at lower edge of D stripe. Sew tops of sleeves (bound-off edges) between markers, easing to fit. Sew side and sleeve seams. ■

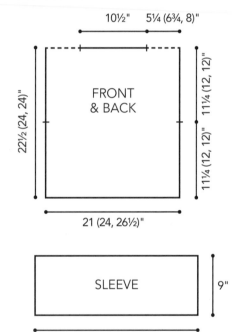

●○○ Sleeveless Shell

This is a standard-fitting shell with a turtleneck collar and A-line shaping.

SIZES
Small, Medium, Large, X-Large, XX-Large and shown in size Small.

KNITTED MEASUREMENTS
• Bust 36½ (40½, 44½, 48½ 52½)"/92.5 (103, 113, 123, 133.5)cm
• Length 25 (25½, 26, 26½, 27)"/63.5 (64.5, 66, 67.5, 68.5)cm

MATERIALS
• 7 (8, 9, 10, 11) 1¾oz/50g balls (each approx 98yd/90m) of Stacy Charles Fine Yarns *Norah* (linen/silk) in #01 oatmeal

• One pair each sizes 9 and 10 (5.5 and 6mm) needles, OR SIZE TO OBTAIN GAUGE

• Size 10 (6mm) circular needle 16"/40cm long

• Stitch markers

• Stitch holders

GAUGE
16 sts and 19 rows = 4"/10cm over St st using size 10 (6mm) needles. TAKE TIME TO CHECK GAUGE.

BACK
With smaller needles, cast on 79 (87, 95, 103, 111) sts.
Row 1 (RS) K1, *p1, k1; rep from * to end.
Row 2 P1, *k1, p1; rep from * to end.
Rep last 2 rows once more. Change to larger needles and work 6 rows in St st (k on RS, p on WS).
Dec row (RS) K2, k2tog, k to last 4 sts, ssk, k2—2 sts dec'd.
Cont in St st, rep dec row every 18th row twice more—73 (81, 89, 97, 105) sts. Work even in St st until piece measures 16"/40.5cm from beg, end with a WS row.

ARMHOLE SHAPING
Dec row 1 (RS) K2, k3tog, k to last 5 sts, k3tog, k2—4 sts dec'd.
Next row K1, purl to last st, k1.
Rep last 2 rows 1 (1, 2, 3, 4) times more—65 (73, 77, 81, 85) sts.
Dec row 2 (RS) K2, k2tog, k to last 4 sts, ssk, k2—2 sts dec'd.
Next row K1, purl to last st, k1.
Rep last 2 rows 4 (6, 6, 6, 6) times more—55 (59, 63, 67, 71) sts.
Cont to work edge st each side in garter st (k every row), work even until armhole measures 8 (8½, 9, 9½, 10)"/20.5 (21.5, 23, 24, 25.5)cm, end with a WS row.

SHOULDER SHAPING
Bind off 6 (7, 8, 8, 9) sts at beg of next 2 rows, 7 (7, 8, 9, 10) sts at beg of next 2 rows. Place rem 29 (31, 31, 33, 33) sts on st holder.

FRONT
Work as for back until armhole measures 5½ (6, 6½, 7, 7½)"/14 (15, 16.5, 18, 19)cm, end with a WS row.

NECK SHAPING
Next row (RS) K18 (19, 21, 22, 24) sts, place next 19 (21, 21, 23, 23) sts on st holder, join 2nd ball of yarn and k to end. Working both sides at once, dec 1 st at neck edge every row 3 times, then every other row twice more—13 (14, 16, 17, 19) sts rem each side. Work even until armhole measures 8 (8½, 9, 9½, 10)"/20.5 (21.5, 23, 24, 25.5)cm, end with a WS row.

SHOULDER SHAPING
Bind off 6 (7, 8, 8, 9) sts at each shoulder edge once, 7 (7, 8, 9, 10) sts once.

FINISHING
Block pieces lightly to measurements. Sew shoulder seams. Sew side seams.

COLLAR
With RS facing and circular needle, beg at left shoulder seam, pick up and k 16 sts along left front neck edge, k19 (21, 21, 23, 23) sts from front neck holder, pick up and k 16 sts along right front neck edge, k29 (31, 31, 33, 33) sts from back neck holder—80 (84, 84, 88, 88) sts. Join and place marker for beg of rnd. Work in St st (k every rnd) until collar measures 8"/20.5cm.
Next 3 rnds *K1, p1; rep from * around. Bind off loosely in rib. ∎

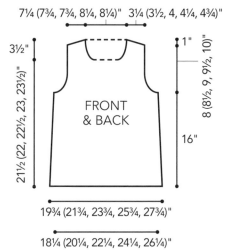

7¼ (7¾, 7¾, 8¼, 8¼)"   3¼ (3½, 4, 4¼, 4¾)"

3½"   1"

21½ (22, 22½, 23, 23½)"   8 (8½, 9, 9½, 10)"

16"

FRONT & BACK

19¾ (21¾, 23¾, 25¾, 27¾)"

18¼ (20¼, 22¼, 24¼, 26¼)"

Turtleneck Tunic

Oversized turtleneck tunic vest with deep side slits and continuing rib trim along the side seams.

SIZES
Sized for Small, Medium, Large, X-Large, 1X, 2X and shown in size Medium.

KNITTED MEASUREMENTS
• Bust 43 (45, 47, 49, 51, 54)"/109 (114, 119, 124.5, 129.5, 137)cm
• Length 31 (31½, 31½, 31½, 32, 32)"/79 (80, 80, 80, 81, 81)cm

MATERIALS
• 5 (6, 6, 6, 7, 7) 3½oz/100g skeins (each approx 197yd/180m) of Cascade Yarns *Eco Duo* (alpaca/wool) in #1701 zebra

• One pair size 8 (5mm) needles, OR SIZE TO OBTAIN GAUGE

• Stitch holder

GAUGE
19 sts and 23 rows = 4"/10cm over St st using size 8 (5mm) needles. TAKE TIME TO CHECK GAUGE.

BACK
Cast on 103 (109, 113, 119, 123, 127) sts.
Row 1 (RS) K1, *p1, k1; rep from * to end.
Row 2 P1, *k1, p1; rep from * to end.
Rep last 2 rows for k1, p1 rib for 7 rows more.
Last row (WS) Work in rib, inc'ing 1 (0, 1, 0, 0, 1) st—104 (109, 114, 119, 123, 128) sts. This ends the side slit.
Row 1 (RS) [K1, p1] 3 times, k92 (97, 102, 107, 111, 116), [p1, k1] 3 times.
Row 2 (WS) [P1, k1] 3 times, p to the last 6 sts, [k1, p1] 3 times.
Rep last 2 rows for St st with rib trim until piece measures 24 (24, 23½, 23, 23, 22½)"/61 (61, 59.5, 58.5, 58.5, 57)cm from beg.

ARMHOLE SHAPING
Bind off 6 (6, 7, 7, 8, 9) sts at beg of next 2 rows, then bind off 2 sts at beg of next 8 (8, 8, 10, 10, 10) rows—76 (81, 84, 85, 87, 90) sts. Work even (in St st only) until armhole measures 7 (7½, 8, 8½, 9, 9½)"/18 (19, 20.5, 21.5, 23, 24)cm. Bind off all sts.

FRONT
Work same as back until armhole measures 5 (5½, 6, 6½, 7, 7½)"/12.5 (14, 15, 16.5, 18, 19)cm.

NECK SHAPING
Next row (RS) K24 (26, 27, 27, 28, 29), place center 28 (29, 30, 31, 31, 32) sts on a st holder, join a 2nd ball of yarn and k to end. Working both sides at once, bind off 1 st from each neck edge 5 times—19 (21, 22, 22, 23, 24) sts rem each side. Work even on sts each side until armhole measures same as back. Bind off sts each side for shoulders.

FINISHING
Sew right shoulder seam.

TURTLENECK
With RS facing, pick up and k 15 sts from shaped left front neck edge, k 28 (29, 30, 31, 31, 32) sts from front holder, pick up and k 15 sts from shaped right front neck edge, pick up and k 33 (34, 35, 36, 36, 37) sts from back neck edge—91 (93, 95, 97, 97, 99) sts.

Row 1 (WS) P1, *k1, p1; rep from * to end.
Row 2 K1, *p1, k1; rep from * to end.
Rep last 2 rows for k1, p1 rib until turtleneck measures 5"/12.5cm.
Bind off sts loosely in rib.
Sew the turtleneck seam and the left shoulder seam (the turtleneck seam should fall to the WS for a turtleneck that is worn against the neck and without folding back).

ARMHOLE TRIMS
With RS facing, pick up and k 79 (85, 91, 95, 101, 107) sts evenly around each armhole edge. Work in k1, p1 rib as for turtleneck for 3 rows.
Bind off sts loosely in rib.
Leaving 10"/25.5cm free for the side slits, sew the side seams, taking some extra sts at the top of the slits for durability in wear. Block very lightly to measurements, avoiding the ribbed areas. ■

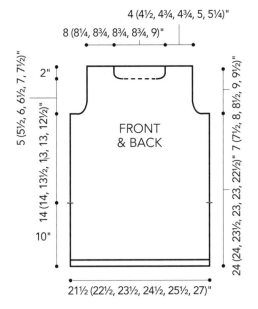

4 (4½, 4¾, 4¾, 5, 5¼)"

8 (8¼, 8¾, 8¾, 8¾, 9)"

2"

5 (5½, 6, 6½, 7, 7½)"

8 (8¼, 8, 8½, 8¾, 9, 9½)"

14 (14, 13½, 13, 13, 12½)"

7 (7½, 8, 8½, 9, 9½)"

FRONT & BACK

10"

24 (24, 23½, 23, 23, 22½)"

21½ (22½, 23½, 24½, 25½, 27)"

— indicates side slits

Garter Cardigan

Oversized garter stitch cardigan with easy shaping, self finished edges and bell shaped sleeves.

SIZES
Sized for Small, Medium, Large, X-Large, 1X and shown in size Medium.

KNITTED MEASUREMENTS
• Bust (closed) 40 (42, 44, 46, 50)"/101.5 (106.5, 111.5, 117, 127)cm
• Length 23 (23½, 24, 25, 25½)"/58.5 (59.5, 61, 63.5, 65)cm
• Upper arm 12 (13, 14, 16, 17)"/30.5 (33, 35.5, 40.5, 43)cm

MATERIALS
• 6 (7, 8, 9, 10) 5oz/140g skeins (each approx 87yd/80m) of Lion Brand Yarns *Wool-Ease Thick & Quick* (acrylic/wool) in #525 wild strawberry
• One pair size 15 (10mm) needles, OR SIZE TO OBTAIN GAUGE

GAUGE
8 sts and 16 rows = 4"/10cm over garter st using size 15 (10mm) needles. TAKE TIME TO CHECK GAUGE.

BACK
Cast on 44 (46, 48, 50, 54) sts.
Work in garter st (k every row) for 30 rows.
Dec row (RS) K1, ssk, k to last 3 sts, k2tog, k1.
Rep dec row 30th row or 7½"/19cm once more—40 (42, 44, 46, 50) sts.
Work even until piece measures 17"/43cm from beg.

ARMHOLE SHAPING
Bind off 4 sts at beg of next 2 rows—32 (34, 36, 38, 42) sts.
Work even until armhole measures 6 (6½, 7, 8, 8½)"/15 (16.5, 18, 20.5, 21.5)cm. Bind off.

LEFT FRONT
Cast on 21 (22, 23, 24, 26) sts.
Row 1 (RS) Knit.
Row 2 (WS) Sl 1 wyif, k to end.

Rep these 2 rows for 28 rows more.
Dec row (RS) K1, ssk, k to end.
Rep dec row every 30th row or 7½"/19cm
once more—19 (20, 21, 22, 24) sts.
Work even until piece measures
16½"/42cm from beg, end with a WS row.

NECK AND ARMHOLE SHAPING
Neck dec row (RS) K to last 3 sts, ssk, k1.
Rep neck dec row (while cont to work the sl
1 wyif at beg of every WS row
for inside front edge) every 6th row 3
(3, 4, 4, 5) times more, AT SAME TIME,
when piece measures 17"/43cm from
beg and there are same number of rows
as back to armhole, bind off 4 sts from
armhole edge on next RS row.
After all neck dec's are completed, work
even on 11 (12, 12, 13, 14) sts until armhole
measures same length as back.
Bind off sts for shoulder.

RIGHT FRONT
Cast on 21 (22, 23, 24, 26) sts.
Row 1 (RS) Sl 1 wyif, k to end.
Row 2 (WS) Knit.
Rep these 2 rows for 28 rows more.
Dec row (RS) Sl 1 wyif, k to last 3 sts,
k2tog, k8.
Rep dec row every 30th row or 7½"/19cm
once more—19 (20, 21, 22, 24) sts.
Work even until piece measures
16½"/42cm from beg.

NECK AND ARMHOLE SHAPING
Neck dec row (RS) Sl 1 wyif, ssk, k to end.
Rep neck dec row every 6th row 3
(3, 4, 4, 5) times more, AT SAME TIME,
when piece measures 17"/43cm from
beg and there are same number of rows
as back to armhole, bind off 4 sts from
armhole edge on next WS row.
After all neck dec's are completed, work
even on 11 (12, 12, 13, 14) sts until
armhole measures same as back.
Bind off sts for shoulder.

SLEEVES
Cast on 28 (30, 32, 36, 38) sts. Work in
garter st for 20 rows.
Dec row (RS) K1, ssk, k to last 3 sts,
k2tog, k1.
Rep dec row every 20th row once more—
24 (26, 28, 32, 34) sts.
Work even until piece measures
14"/35.5cm from beg. Bind off.

FINISHING
Block pieces lightly to measurements.
Sew shoulder seams. Sew sleeves into
armholes. Sew the top 2"/5cm of sleeve
to the underarm sleeve bind-offs.
Sew side and sleeve seams. ■

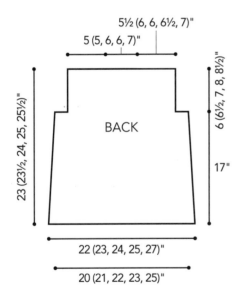
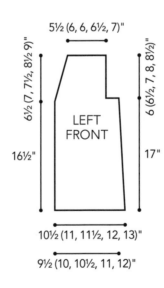
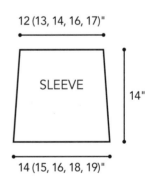

●●○ Hat & Cowl Set

Waffle-stitch cowl and hat with contrasting edges.

SIZE
Sized for adult woman.

KNITTED MEASUREMENTS
HAT
• Brim circumference 20¾"/52.5cm
• Length (unfolded) 10"/25.5cm

COWL
• Circumference 36"/91.5cm
• Width 12"/30.5cm

MATERIALS
Note: If making both hat and cowl,
4 hanks in MC and 1 hank in CC
is sufficient for both projects.

HAT
• 2 1¾oz/50g hanks (each approx
164yd/150m) of Blue Sky Fibers *Eco
Cashmere* (recycled cashmere/virgin
cashmere) in #1803 mineral bath (MC)

• 1 hank in #1807 gold rush (CC)

• Size 7 (4.5mm) circular needle
16"/40cm long, OR SIZE TO OBTAIN
GAUGE

• One set (5) each size 7 (4.5mm)
double-pointed needles (dpn)

• Stitch markers

COWL
• 3 1¾oz/50g hanks in #1803
mineral bath (MC)

• 1 hank in #1807 gold rush (CC)

• Size 7 (4.5mm) circular needle
24"/60cm long, OR SIZE TO OBTAIN
GAUGE

• Stitch markers

GAUGE
20 sts and 30 rnds = 4"/10cm over waffle
stitch using size 7 (4.5mm) needles.
TAKE TIME TO CHECK GAUGE.

WAFFLE STITCH
(multiple of 4 sts)
Rnd 1 Purl.
Rnds 2 and 3 *P2, k2; rep from * around.
Rnd 4 Knit.
Rep rnds 1–4 for waffle stitch.

NOTE
Hat can be worn with brim folded for a
more traditional fit, or unfolded for
a slouchy fit.

HAT
With circular needle and CC, cast on 104
sts. Join, taking care not to twist sts, and
place marker (pm) for beg of rnd.
Rnd 1 *K2, p2; rep from * around.
Rep last rnd once more for k2, p2 rib.
Cut CC and join MC, cont in k2,
p2 rib for 6 rnds more.

BEG WAFFLE STITCH
Work in waffle stitch until piece measures
8½"/21.5cm from beg, placing markers on
last rnd as foll: work 7 sts in pat, pm, [work
8 sts in pat, pm] 12 times, work last st.

CROWN SHAPING
Note Change to dpn when sts no longer fit
comfortably on circular needle.
Dec rnd *Work in pat to marker, sl marker,
ssk; rep from * around, removing beg
of rnd marker and replacing after last
ssk—13 sts dec'd.
Next rnd Work even in pat.
Rep last 2 rnds 3 times more—52 sts. Rep
dec rnd every rnd 3 times more—13 sts.
Remove markers.

Next rnd K1, [ssk] 6 times—7 sts.
Cut yarn and pull through rem sts,
draw up and secure.

COWL
With CC and circular needle, cast on
180 sts. Join, taking care not to twist sts,
and place marker (pm) for beg of rnd.
Rnd 1 *K2, p2; rep from * around.
Rep last rnd once more for k2, p2 rib.
Cut CC and join MC, cont in k2,
p2 rib for 6 rnds more.

BEG WAFFLE STITCH
Work in waffle stitch until piece measures
approx 10¾"/27.5cm from beg.
With MC, work 6 rnds in k2, p2 rib.
Cut MC and join CC, cont in k2,
p2 rib for 2 rnds more.
With CC, bind off in rib.

FINISHING
Block lightly to measurements. ■

●●○ Lace Cowl

A cozy cowl is knitted in the round in a delicate lace pattern.

KNITTED MEASUREMENTS
- Circumference 28"/71cm
- Length 11½"/29cm

MATERIALS

ORIGINAL YARN

- 2 1¾ oz/50g balls (each approx 98yd/90m) of Bergère de France *Mohair* (mohair/polyamide/wool) in #243.22 souffle

SUBSTITUTE YARN
- 2 1¾ oz/50g balls (each approx 66yd/60m) of Bergère de France *Plume* (combed wool/acrylic/polyamide) in orge

- Size 9 (5.5mm) circular needle, 24"/60cm long
OR SIZE TO OBTAIN GAUGE

- Stitch marker

GAUGE
14 sts and 25 rnds = 4"/10cm over lace pat using size 9 (5.5mm) needle.
TAKE TIME TO CHECK GAUGE.

LACE PATTERN
(multiple of 7 sts)
Rnd 1 *K1, k2tog, yo, k1, yo, ssk, k1; rep from * around.
Rnds 2 and 4 Knit.
Rnd 3 *K2tog, yo, k3, yo, ssk; rep from * around.
Rep rnds 1–4 for lace pattern.

COWL
Cast on 98 sts. Join for working in the round and pm, taking care not to twist sts. Work in lace pat for 11½"/29cm, end with a row 4. Bind off loosely. ■

●●○ Textured Wrap

A combination of different knit and purl stitch patterns create texture in this easy-to-make wrap.

KNITTED MEASUREMENTS
- Width approx 14½"/37cm
- Length 60"/153cm

MATERIALS
- 7 2¼oz/65g balls (each approx 142yd/130m) of Cleckheaton Australian *Superfine Merino* (wool) in #35 iceberg
- One pair size 6 (4mm) needles, OR SIZE TO OBTAIN GAUGE

GAUGES
- 24 sts and 34 rows = 4"/10cm over section 1 pat using size 6 (4mm) needles.
- 23 sts and 46 rows = 4"/10cm over garter st using size 6 (4mm) needles. TAKE TIME TO CHECK GAUGES.

WRAP
Cast on 89 sts.

BEG SECTION 1
Row 1 (RS) K4, *yo, SK2P, yo, k3; rep from * to last 7 sts, yo, SK2P, yo, k4.
Rows 2 and 4 P4, *k3, p3; rep from * to last 4 sts, p4.
Row 3 K4, *p3, k3; rep from * to last 4 sts, k4.
Row 5 K2, k2tog, yo, *k3, yo, SK2P, yo; rep from * to last 7 sts, k3, yo, SKP, k2.
Row 6 K4, *p3, k3; rep from * to last 4 sts, k4.
Row 7 P4, *k3, p3, rep from * to last 4 sts, p4.
Row 8 Rep row 6.
Rep rows 1–8 until section 1 measures 10"/25.5cm, end with a pat row 6.
Next row (RS) Knit and dec 5 sts evenly across—84 sts.

BEG SECTION 2
Work in garter st (knit every row) until section 2 measures 10"/25.5cm, end with a WS row.
Next row (RS) Knit and inc 5 sts evenly across—89 sts.
Next row Purl.

BEG SECTION 3
Row 1 (RS) P7, *p2tog, yo, k1, yo, p2tog, p2; rep from * to last 12 sts, p2tog, yo, k1, yo, p2tog, p7.
Row 2 Purl.
Row 3 Knit.
Row 4 Purl.
Rep rows 1–4 rows until section 3 measures 10"/25.5cm, end with a pat row 4.

BEG SECTION 4
Row 1 (RS) K4, *p3, k3; rep from * to last 7 sts, p3, k4.
Rows 2 and 3 P4, *k3, p3; rep from * to last 7 sts, k3, p4.
Row 4 Rep row 1.
Rep rows 1–4 rows until section 4 measures 10"/25.5cm, end with pat row 4.
Next row (RS) Knit and dec 5 sts evenly across—84 sts.
Next row Knit.

BEG SECTION 5
Rows 1–4 Knit.
Row 5 (RS) K1, *yo, k2tog; rep from * to end.
Row 6 Knit.
Rep rows 1–6 rows until section 5 measures 10"/25.5cm, end with a pat row 6. Knit 3 rows.
Next row (WS) Knit and inc 5 sts evenly across—89 sts.

BEG SECTION 6
Row 1 (RS) K1, *p1, k1; rep from * to end.
Row 2 P1, *k1, p1; rep from * to end.
Rows 3–6 Knit.
Rep rows 1–6 until section 6 measures 10"/25.5cm, end with a pat row 6. Bind off.

FINISHING
Block lightly to measurements. ■

●●○ Scarf & Headband

Scarf and matching adjustable headband knit in reversible garter stitch.

KNITTED MEASUREMENTS
- Headband width 4½"/11.5cm
- Scarf width 8"/20.5cm
- Scarf Length (from point to point) approx 40"/101.5cm

MATERIALS
- 4 1¾oz/50g balls (each approx 109yd/100m) of Valley Yarns *Amherst* (merino wool) in light grey
- One pair size 8 (5mm) needles OR SIZE TO OBTAIN GAUGE
- One ring ¾"/2cm (inside diameter) for headband

GAUGE
20 sts and 40 rows = 4"/10cm over garter st using size 8 (5mm) needles. TAKE TIME TO CHECK GAUGE.

SCARF
Cast on 2 sts.

INCREASE POINT
Row 1 K1, yo, k1—3 sts.
Row 2 Kfb, k2—4 sts.
Row 3 Kfb, knit to end—1 st inc'd.
Cont to inc 1 st at beg of every row until there are 40 sts total.

MAIN SCARF
Next row Sl 1 purlwise, knit to end.
Rep last row (slipping first st of every row for selvage sts) until piece measures 36"/94cm from beg, or 4"/10cm less than desired length.

DECREASE POINT
Row 1 Sl 1 purlwise, k2tog, knit to end—1 st dec'd.
Rep last row until 3 sts rem.
Last row Sl 1 purlwise, k2tog, pass slip st over k2tog. Fasten off last st.

HEADBAND
Cast on 3 sts.

INCREASE POINT
Beg with row 3, work as for Increase Point for scarf until there are 22 sts.

MAIN HEADBAND
Work in garter stitch as for scarf until piece measures approx 21"/53.5cm from beg, or 2¼"/5.5cm less than desired length.

DECREASE POINT
Work as for scarf until 3 sts rem.
Last row Sl 1 purlwise, k2tog, pass slip st over k2tog. Fasten off last st.

FINISHING
Do not block.

Pass both pointed ends of headband through ring to fit desired head size. Arrange ends folding them to sides, once ends are pulled through ring. Points will hug band due to pattern of decreases.

Note: Yarn may be used to join ends, and pointed ends may be sewn to band, if you prefer. This will prevent band from being adjustable). ■

●●○ Short-Sleeve Pullover & Scarf

Classic fit short-sleeve pullover with ribbed trims and matching ribbed scarf.

SIZES
Sized for X-Small, Small, Medium, Large, 1X, 2X and shown in size X-Small.

KNITTED MEASUREMENTS
PULLOVER
• Bust 33 (37, 41, 45, 49, 53)"/84 (94, 104, 114.5, 124.5, 134.5)cm
• Length 22 (22½, 23, 23½, 24, 24½)"/56 (57, 58.5, 59.5, 61, 62)cm
• Upper arm 11¾ (12¼, 12¼, 13, 13½, 14)"/30 (31, 31, 33, 34.5, 35.5)cm

SCARF
• Width 8"/20cm
• Length 62"/157.5cm

MATERIALS
• 6 (7, 7, 8, 8, 9) 1¾oz/50g balls (each approx 143yds/130m) of Tahki Yarns *Everest* (alpaca/polyamide/wool) in #11 merlot
• One pair each size 9 and 10 (5.5 and 6mm) needles, OR SIZE TO OBTAIN GAUGE
• One size 9 (5.5mm) circular needle, 16"/40cm long
• Stitch holders
• Stitch marker

GAUGES
• 15 sts and 22 rows to 4"/10cm over St st using size 10 (6mm) needles.
• 16 sts and 22 rows to 4"/10cm over k2, p2 rib using size 10 (6mm) needles.
TAKE TIME TO CHECK GAUGES.

PULLOVER
BACK
With smaller needles, cast on 66 (74, 82, 90, 98, 106) sts.
Row 1 (RS) K2, *p2, k2: rep from * to end.
Row 2 (WS) P2, *k2, p2; rep from * to end.
Rep these 2 rows for k2, p2 rib until piece measures 3"/7.5cm from beg, end with a WS row.
Change to larger needles.
Next row (RS) Knit, dec'ing 4 (4, 5, 6, 6, 6) sts evenly across—62 (70, 77, 84, 92, 100) sts.

Cont even in St st (k on RS, p on WS) until piece measures 14"/35.5cm from beg.

ARMHOLE SHAPING
Bind off 2 (2, 3, 3, 3, 3) sts at beg of next 2 rows, 2 sts at beg of next 2 (2, 2, 2, 2, 4) rows. Dec 1 st each side every other row 2 (3, 3, 5, 6, 6) times—50 (56, 61, 64, 70, 74) sts.
Work even until armhole measures 7 (7½, 8, 8½, 9, 9½)"/18 (19, 20, 21.5, 23, 24)cm.

SHOULDER SHAPING
Bind off 4 (4, 5, 5, 6, 7) sts at beg of next 4 rows, 3 (5, 5, 6, 7, 6) sts at beg of next 2 rows. Leave rem 28 (30, 31, 32, 32, 34) sts on holder for back neck.

FRONT
Work same as back until armhole measures 3½ (4, 4½, 5, 5½, 6)"/9 (10, 11.5, 12.5, 14, 15)cm.

NECK SHAPING
Next row (RS) K19 (21, 23, 24, 27, 29) sts, sl center 12 (14, 15, 16, 16, 16) sts to st holder, join a 2nd ball of yarn and k rem 19 (21, 23, 24, 27, 29) sts.
Working both sides at once, dec 1 st at each neck edge every row 5 times, then every RS row 3 (3, 3, 3, 3, 4) times—11 (13, 15, 16, 19, 20) sts each side.
Work even until armhole measures same as back.

SHOULDER SHAPING
Bind off from each shoulder edge 4 (4, 5, 5, 6, 7) sts twice, 3 (5, 5, 6, 7, 6) sts once.

SLEEVES
With smaller needles, cast on 42 (42, 42, 46, 46, 50) sts. Work in k2, p2 rib for 6 rows.
Change to larger needles.
Next row (RS) Knit, dec'ing 2 (0, 0, 2, 0, 2) sts evenly across—40 (42, 42, 44, 46, 48) sts.
Cont in St st (k on RS, p on WS), inc 1 st each side of every 8th row twice—44 (46, 46, 48, 50, 52) sts. Work even until piece measures 4½ (5, 5, 5½, 5½, 6)"/11.5 (12.5, 12.5, 14, 14, 15)cm from beg.

CAP SHAPING
Bind off 2 (2, 3, 3, 3, 3) sts at beg of next 2 rows, 2 sts at beg of next 2 rows. Dec 1 st each side every RS row 2 (3, 2, 3, 4, 5) times, every 4th row 3 (3, 4, 4, 4, 4) times, then every RS row 2 (2, 1, 1, 1, 1) time(s). Bind off 2 sts at beg of next 2 rows, 3 sts at beg of next 2 rows. Bind off rem 12 sts.

FINISHING
Block pieces to measurements. Sew shoulder seams.

NECKBAND
With RS facing and circular needle, pick up and k 76 (80, 80, 84, 84, 88) sts evenly around neck opening.
Join and pm for beg of rnd.
Rnd 1 *K2, p2; rep from * around.
Rep rnd 1 twice more. Bind off sts in pat.
Sew side and sleeve seams. Set in sleeve. ■

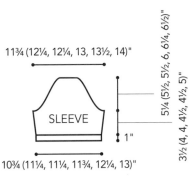

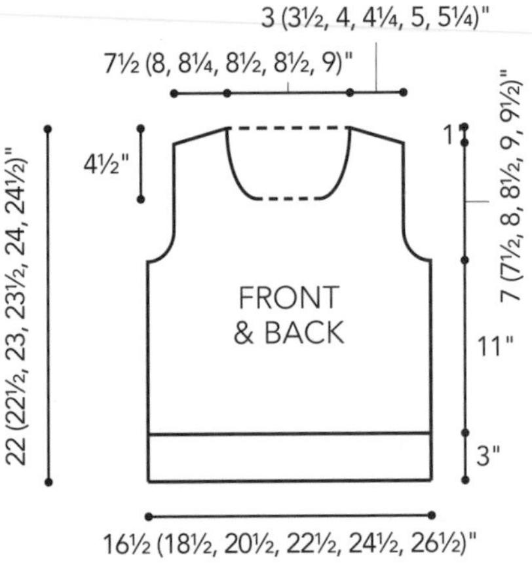

3 (3½, 4, 4¼, 5, 5¼)"
7½ (8, 8¼, 8½, 8½, 9)"
4½"
22 (22½, 23, 23½, 24, 24½)"
7 (7½, 8, 8½, 9, 9½)"
11"
1"
3"
FRONT & BACK
16½ (18½, 20½, 22½, 24½, 26½)"

11¾ (12¼, 12¼, 13, 13½, 14)"
5¼ (5½, 5½, 6, 6¼, 6½)"
SLEEVE
1"
3½ (4, 4, 4½, 4½, 5)"
10¾ (11¼, 11¼, 11¾, 12¼, 13)"

SCARF
With larger needles, cast on 34 sts.
Row 1 Sl 1 wyif, *k2, p2; rep from * to last st, k1.
Rep row 1 until piece measures 62"/157.5cm from beg. Bind off in rib.

FINISHING
Block to measurements. ■

●●○ Drop-Shoulder Pullover

Oversized pullover with deep ribbed trims, square armholes and dropped shoulders.

SIZES
Sized for Small, Medium, Large, X-Large, XX-Large, 1X, 2X and shown in size Small.

KNITTED MEASUREMENTS
• Bust 42 (44½, 46, 48, 49½, 53, 56½)"/106.5 (113, 117, 122, 125.5, 134.5, 143.5)cm
• Length 27 (27½, 27½, 27½, 28, 28, 28½)"/68.5 (70, 70, 70, 71, 71, 72.5)cm
• Upper arm 16 (17, 18, 19, 20, 21, 22)"/40.5 (43, 45.5, 48, 51, 53, 56)cm

MATERIALS
• 6 (7, 7, 8, 8, 9, 9) 3½oz/100g hanks (each approx 218yd/200m) of Cascade Yarns *Cantata* (cotton/wool) in #5 brown
• One pair each sizes 7 and 9 (4.5 and 5.5mm) needles, OR SIZE TO OBTAIN GAUGE
• Size 7 (4.5mm) circular needle, 16"/40cm long
• Stitch holders and removable st markers

GAUGE
17 sts and 24 rows = 4"/10cm over St st using larger needles.
TAKE TIME TO CHECK GAUGE.

NOTE
One St st selvage st is worked on all edges of the pieces and these sts are not figured into the finished measurements.

BACK
With smaller needles, cast on 121 (127, 131, 137, 141, 151, 161) sts.
Row 1 (RS) K1, *p1, k1; rep from * to end.
Row 2 (WS) P1, *k1, p1; rep from * to end.
Rep these 2 rows for k1, p1 rib until piece measures 6"/15cm from beg, end with a WS row.
Change to larger needles.
Next row (RS) K3 (4, 4, 3, 3, 4, 3), [k2tog, k2] 28 (29, 30, 32, 33, 35, 38) times, k2tog, k4 (5, 5, 4, 4, 5, 4)—92 (97, 100, 104, 107, 115, 122) sts.
Beg with a purl row, work even in St st until piece measures 18 (18, 17½, 17, 17, 16½, 16½)"/45.5 (45.5, 44.5, 43, 43, 42, 42)cm from beg.

ARMHOLE SHAPING
Bind off 4 sts at beg of next 2 rows—84 (89, 92, 96, 99, 107, 114) sts. Work even until armhole measures 8 (8½, 9, 9½, 10, 10½, 11)"/20.5 (21.5, 23, 24, 25.5, 26.5, 28)cm.

SHOULDER SHAPING
Next row (RS) Bind off 7 (7, 7, 9, 8, 9, 11) sts, k until there are 21 (23, 24, 24, 26, 29, 30) sts on needle, join a 2nd ball of yarn and k next 28 (29, 30, 30, 31, 31, 32) sts, place these sts on holder, k to end.
Next row (WS) Bind off 7 (7, 7, 9, 8, 9, 11) sts, p to end of first side; on 2nd side, p rem 21 (23, 24, 24, 26, 29, 30) sts. Working both sides at once, bind off 7 (7, 8, 8, 8, 9, 10) sts from each shoulder edge 3 (1, 3, 3, 1, 1, 3) times more, then 0 (8, 0, 0, 9, 10, 0) sts 0 (2, 0, 1, 2, 2, 0) times more.

FRONT
Work same as back, including armhole shaping, until armhole measures 6 (6½, 7, 7½, 8, 8½, 9)"/15 (16.5, 18, 19, 20.5, 21.5, 23)cm

NECK SHAPING
Next row (RS) K37 (39, 40, 42, 43, 47, 50), join a 2nd ball of yarn and k next 10 (11, 12, 12, 13, 13, 14) sts and sl these sts to a holder, join 2nd ball of yarn and k rem 37 (39, 40, 42, 43, 47, 50) sts. Working both sides at once, bind off 4 sts from each neck edge once, then 2 sts from each neck edge once.
Dec row (RS) K to the last 3 sts of first side, k2tog, k1; on 2nd side, k1, SKP, k to end. Rep this dec row every other row twice more—28 (30, 31, 33, 34, 38, 41) sts rem each side.
Work even until armhole measures same as back.

SHOULDER SHAPING
Bind off 7 (7, 7, 9, 8, 9, 11) sts from each shoulder edge 4 (2, 1, 1, 2, 2, 1) times, then 0 (8, 8, 8, 9, 10, 10) sts 0 (2, 3, 3, 2, 2, 3) times.

SLEEVES

With smaller needles, cast on 57
(57, 63, 65, 69, 71, 73) sts. Work in k1,
p1 rib as on back for 5"/12.5cm.
Change to larger needles.
Next row (RS) K3 (3, 3, 3, 1, 3, 3),
[k2tog, k2] 13 (13, 15, 15, 17, 17, 17) times,
k2 (2, 0, 2, 0, 0, 2)—44 (44, 48, 50,
52, 54, 56) sts.
Beg with a purl row, work in St st
for 3 rows more.
Inc row (RS) K1, knit in front and back
of next st (kfb), k to last 2 sts, end kfb, k1.
Rep inc row every 6th row 12
(8, 8, 6, 4, 2, 0) times more, then
every 4th row 0 (6, 6, 9, 12, 15, 18)
times—70 (74, 78, 82, 86, 90, 94) sts.
Work even for 1"/2.5cm more OR until
piece measures 19½"/49.5cm from beg.
Bind off.

FINISHING

Sew shoulder seams. Pm at 1"/2.5cm
down from top of sleeve. Center sleeves
at shoulder seams and sew to armhole
openings, then sew last 1"/2.5cm from the
markers to 4 bound-off sts at armholes.
Sew side and sleeve seams.

NECKBAND

With RS facing and circular needle, pick
up and k 5 sts from right side of back neck,
k28 (29, 30, 30, 31, 31, 32) sts from back
neck holder, pick up and k 5 sts from left
side of back neck, 18 sts from shaped front
neck edge, k10 (11, 12, 12, 13, 13, 14) sts
from front neck holder, pick up and
k 18 sts from shaped front neck edge—84
(86, 88, 88, 90, 90, 92) sts.
Join to work in rnds and pm to mark
beg of rnds. Work in St st (k every rnd)
for 1¾"/4.5cm. Bind off loosely using
larger needles.
Block finished piece lightly on the WS. ■

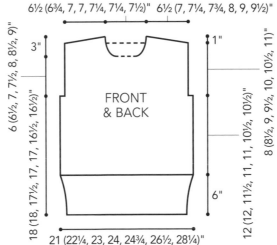

6½ (6¾, 7, 7, 7¼, 7¼, 7½)"   6½ (7, 7¼, 7¾, 8, 9, 9½)"

3"

1"

6 (6½, 7, 7½, 8, 8½, 9)"

FRONT & BACK

8 (8½, 9, 9½, 10, 10½, 11)"

18 (18, 17½, 17, 17, 16½, 16½)"

12 (12, 11½, 11, 11, 10½, 10½)"

6"

21 (22¼, 23, 24, 24¾, 26½, 28¼)"

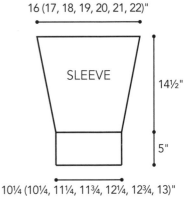

16 (17, 18, 19, 20, 21, 22)"

SLEEVE

14½"

5"

10¼ (10¼, 11¼, 11¾, 12¼, 12¾, 13)"

●●○ Chunky Cardigan

Oversized jacket worked in stockinette stitch with deep garter stitch borders and garter stitch collar.

SIZES
Sized for Small, Medium, Large and X-Large and shown in size Medium.

KNITTED MEASUREMENTS
- Bust 40 (45½, 50½, 56)"/101.5 (115.5, 128, 142)cm
- Length 28 (30, 30, 30)"/71 (76, 76, 76)cm
- Upper arm 12½ (13½, 14½, 15½)"/31.5 (34.5, 37, 39.5)cm

MATERIALS
- 8 (9, 10, 11) 3½oz/100g hanks (each approx 110yd/100m) of Plymouth Yarn Company *Baby Alpaca Grande* (baby alpaca) in #7754 green heather
- One pair size 10½ (6.5mm) needles OR SIZE TO OBTAIN GAUGE
- Size K-10½ (6.5mm) crochet hook (optional)
- Stitch markers
- Stitch holders

GAUGES
- 12 sts and 17 rows = 4"/10cm over St st using size 10½ (6.5mm) needles.
- 12 sts and 25 rows = 4"/10cm over garter st using size 10½ (6.5mm) needles.

TAKE TIME TO CHECK GAUGES.

STITCH GLOSSARY
M1 p-st Insert needle from front to back under the strand between the last st worked and the next st on the LH needle. Purl into the back loop to inc one st.

NOTE
One stitch each side is used in seaming and not counted in schematic measurements.

BACK
Note Read before beg to knit.
Cast on 56 (64, 72, 80) sts.
Beg with a WS row, work in garter st (k every row) for 56 rows (28 ridges on RS, piece measures approx 9"/23cm), end with a RS row, AT SAME TIME, inc 1 st each side every 4"/10cm twice—60 (68, 76, 84) sts. Work in St st (k on RS, p on WS), inc'ing at each side edge once more 4"/10cm from last inc—62 (70, 78, 86) sts.
Cont in St st until piece measures 20¼ (21¾, 21¼, 20¾)"/51.5 (55, 54, 52.5)cm from beg, end with a WS row and place markers (pm) for armhole each side of last row.

Cont in St st until piece measures 6¼ (6¾, 7¼, 7¾)"/16 (17, 18.5, 19.5)cm from markers, end with a WS row.

SHOULDER SHAPING
Bind off 6 (7, 8, 9) sts at beg of next 6 rows. Place rem 26 (28, 30, 32) sts on st holder for back neck.

LEFT FRONT
Note Read before beg to knit.
Cast on 28 (32, 36, 40) sts.
Beg with a WS row, work in garter st for 56 rows (28 ridges on RS, piece measures approx 9"/23cm), end with a RS

row, AT SAME TIME, inc 1 st at side edge (beg of RS rows) every 4"/10cm twice—30 (34, 38, 42) sts.
Next row (WS) Purl.
Next row (RS) K to last 3 sts, [M1 p-st, k1] 3 times—33 (37, 41, 45) sts.
Next row (WS) K2, [p1, k1] twice, (6-st ribbed front edge), p to end.
Next row (RS) K to last 6 sts, [p1, k1] 3 times.
Cont in St st, working 6-st ribbed front edge as established, inc 1 st at side edge once more 4"/10cm from last inc—34 (38, 42, 46) sts.
Cont in St st with ribbed front edge until piece measures 20¼ (21¾, 21¼, 20¾)"/51.5 (55, 54, 52.5)cm from beg, end with a WS row and pm for armhole at side edge of last row worked.
Cont in St st until piece measures 3¾ (4¼, 4¾, 5¼)"/9.5 (11, 12, 13.5)cm from marker, end with a RS row.

NECK AND SHOULDER SHAPING
Bind off 6 sts at neck edge (beg of WS rows) once, 3 (3, 4, 4) sts once, 3 (3, 3, 4) sts once, then dec 1 st at neck edge every other row 4 (5, 5, 5) times, AT SAME TIME, when armhole measures same as back to shoulder, end with a WS row and bind off 6 (7, 8, 9) sts at shoulder edge (beg of RS rows) 3 times.

RIGHT FRONT
Note Read before beg to knit.
Cast on 28 (32, 36, 40) sts.
Beg with a WS row, work in garter st (k every row) for 56 rows (28 ridges on RS, piece measures approx 9"/23cm), end with a RS row, AT SAME TIME, inc 1 st at

side edge (end of RS rows) every 4"/10cm twice—30 (34, 38, 42) sts.
Next row (WS) Purl.
Next row (RS) [K1, M1 p-st] 3 times, k to end—33 (37, 41, 45) sts.
Next row (WS) P to last 6 sts, [k1, p1] twice, k2 (6-st ribbed front edge).
Next row (RS) [K1, p1] 3 times, k to end.
Cont in St st, working 6-st ribbed front edge as established, inc 1 st at side edge once more 4"/10cm from last inc—34 (38, 42, 46) sts.
Cont in St st with ribbed front edge until piece measures 20¼ (21¾, 21¼, 20¾)"/51.5 (55, 54, 52.5)cm from beg, end with a WS row and pm for armhole at side edge of last row worked.
Cont in St st until piece measures 3¾ (4¼, 4¾, 5¼)"/9.5 (11, 12, 13.5)cm from marker, end with a WS row.

NECK AND SHOULDER SHAPING
Bind off 6 sts at neck edge (beg of RS rows) once, 3 (3, 4, 4) sts once, 3 (3, 3, 4) sts once, then dec 1 st at neck edge every other row 4 (5, 5, 5) times, AT SAME TIME, when armhole measures same as back to shoulder, end with a RS row and bind off 6 (7, 8, 9) sts at shoulder edge (beg of WS rows) 3 times.

SLEEVES
Note Read before beg to knit.
Cast on 26 (28, 28, 30) sts.
Beg with a WS row, work in garter st (k every row) for 32 rows (16 ridges on RS, piece measures approx 5"/12.5cm), end with a RS row, AT SAME TIME, when piece measures 4"/10cm from beg, inc 1 st each side—28 (30, 30, 32) sts.

Work 2 rows in St st.
Cont in St st, inc 1 st at each side on next row, then every 8th (8th, 6th, 6th) row 4 (5, 7, 7) times more—38 (42, 46, 48) sts.
Work even until piece measures 18"/45.5cm from beg, end with a WS row. Bind off.

FINISHING
Sew shoulder seams. Sew upper edges of sleeves between armhole markers. Sew sleeve and side seams.

COLLAR
With RS facing, beg at right front neck edge at first st after bound-off 6-st ribbed front edge, pick up and k 18 sts along shaped right front neck to shoulder, pm, k 26 (28, 30, 32) sts from back neck holder, pm, pick up and k 18 sts along shaped left front neck edge, ending at last st before bound-off 6-st ribbed front edge—62 (64, 66, 68) sts.
Knit 4 rows.
Next row K1, M1, k to marker, sl marker, M1, k to marker, M1, sl marker, k to last st, M1, k1—66 (68, 70, 72) sts.
Knit 4 rows.
Next row K1, M1, k to center back, M1, k to last st, M1, k1—69 (71, 73, 75) sts.
Knit 6 rows.
Next row K1, M1, k to marker, sl marker, M1, k to marker, M1, sl marker, k to last st, M1, k1—73 (75, 77, 79) sts.
Knit 8 rows.
Next row K1, M1, k to marker, sl marker, M1, k to marker, M1, sl marker, k to last st, M1, k1—77 (79, 81, 83) sts.
Knit 4 rows. Bind off. ■

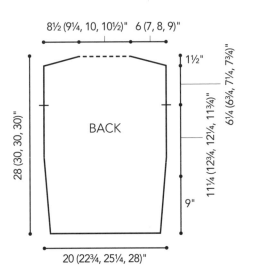

8½ (9¼, 10, 10½)" 6 (7, 8, 9)"
1½"
6¼ (6¾, 7¼, 7¾)"
BACK
28 (30, 30, 30)"
11¼ (12¾, 12¼, 11¾)"
9"
20 (22¾, 25¼, 28)"

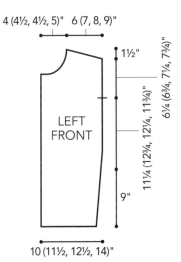

4 (4½, 4½, 5)" 6 (7, 8, 9)"
1½"
6¼ (6¾, 7¼, 7¾)"
LEFT FRONT
11¼ (12¾, 12¼, 11¾)"
9"
10 (11½, 12½, 14)"

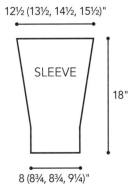

12½ (13½, 14½, 15½)"
SLEEVE
18"
8 (8¾, 8¾, 9¼)"

●●○ Simple Pullover

This standard-fitting pullover, knitted with soft baby alpaca, has a self-finished hemline.

SIZES
Sized for X-Small, Small, Medium, Large, X-Large, XX-Large, 1X, 2X and shown in size Small.

KNITTED MEASUREMENTS

- Bust 34 (36½, 39½, 41, 43½, 46, 49, 52)"/86 (92.5, 100, 104, 110.5, 117, 124.5, 132)cm
- Length 23 (23½, 24, 24½, 25, 25, 25½, 26)"/58.5 (59.5, 61, 62, 63.5, 63.5, 65, 66)cm
- Upper arm 12 (12½, 13½, 14, 15, 15½, 16, 16¾)"/30.5 (32, 34, 35.5, 38, 39.5, 40.5, 42.5)cm

MATERIALS

- 4 (4, 5, 5, 6, 6, 7, 7) 1¾oz/50g balls (each approx 110yd/100m) of Plymouth Yarn Company *Baby Alpaca Brush* (alpaca/acrylic) in #6307 light gray
- One pair size 11 (8mm) needles OR SIZE TO OBTAIN GAUGE
- One size 11 (8mm) circular needle, 16"/40cm long
- Stitch holders

GAUGE
10½ sts and 13 rows = 4"/10cm over St st using size 11 (8mm) needles.
TAKE TIME TO CHECK GAUGE.

NOTE
One selvage st is worked at each edge and does not figure into the schematic or finished measurements.

BACK
Cast on 47 (50, 53, 56, 59, 62, 66, 70) sts. Beg with a (WS) purl row, work in St st for 15½ (15½, 15½, 15½, 15½, 15, 15, 15)"/39.5 (39.5, 39.5, 39.5, 39.5, 38, 38, 38)cm.

ARMHOLE SHAPING
Bind off 4 (4, 4, 4, 4, 4, 5, 5) sts at beg of next 2 rows.
Dec row (RS) K1, SKP, k to last 3 sts, k2tog, k1. Rep dec row every other row 2 (2, 2, 2, 2, 3, 3, 4) times more—33 (36, 39, 42, 45, 46, 48, 50) sts.
Work even until armhole measures 7½ (8, 8½, 9, 9½, 10, 10½, 11)"/19 (20.5, 21.5, 23, 24, 25.5, 26.5, 28)cm.
Next row (RS) Bind off 9 (10, 11, 12, 13, 13, 14, 15) sts for shoulder, join a 2nd ball of yarn and k next 15 (16, 17, 18, 19, 20, 20, 20) sts and sl these sts to a st holder for neck, bind off last 9 (10, 11, 12, 13, 13, 14, 15) sts for shoulder.

FRONT
Work as for back until armhole measures 5½ (6, 6½, 7, 7½, 8, 8½, 9)"/14 (15, 16.5, 18, 19, 20.5, 21.5, 23)cm.

NECK SHAPING
Next row (RS) K11 (12, 13, 14, 15, 15, 16, 17) sts, sl the center 11 (12, 13, 14, 15, 16, 16, 16) sts to a st holder, join a 2nd ball of yarn and k to end. Working both sides at once, dec 1 st each side of neck every other row twice. When piece measures same as back, bind off rem 9 (10, 11, 12, 13, 13, 14, 15) sts each side for shoulders.

SLEEVES
Cast on 21 (21, 23, 23, 25, 25, 26, 28) sts. Beg with a (WS) purl row, work in St st for 9 rows.
Inc row (RS) K1, kfb, k to the last 3 sts, kfb, k2. Rep inc row every 10th row 4 (2, 2, 1, 1, 0, 0, 0) times more then every 6th row 1 (4, 4, 6, 6, 8, 8, 8) times—33 (35, 37, 39, 41, 43, 44, 46) sts.
Work even until piece measures 18"/45.5cm from beg.

CAP SHAPING
Bind off 4 (4, 4, 4, 4, 4, 5, 5) sts at beg of next 2 rows.
Dec row (RS) K1, SKP, k to last 3 sts, k2tog, k1. Rep dec row every other row 5 (6, 7, 8, 9, 10, 11, 12) times more. Bind off 3 sts at beg of next 2 rows. Bind off rem 7 (7, 7, 7, 7, 7, 4, 4) sts.

FINISHING
Sew shoulder seams. Set in sleeves. Sew side and sleeve seams.

NECKBAND
With RS facing and circular needle, k 15 (16, 17, 18, 19, 20, 20, 20) sts from back neck holder, pick up and k 10 sts from shaped neck edge, k 11 (12, 13, 14, 15, 16, 16, 16) sts from front neck, pick up and k 10 sts from shaped neck edge—46 (48, 50, 52, 54, 56, 56, 56) sts. Join to work in rnds and pm to mark beg of rnds.
Knit 2 rnds. Bind off purlwise. ■

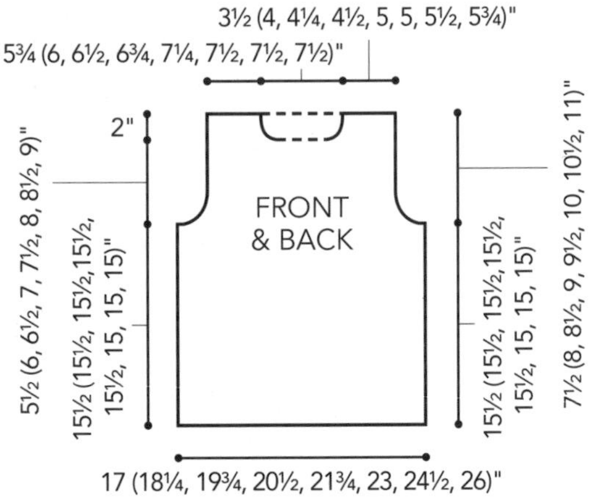
3½ (4, 4¼, 4½, 5, 5, 5½, 5¾)"
5¾ (6, 6½, 6¾, 7¼, 7½, 7½, 7½)"
2"
5½ (6, 6½, 7, 7½, 8, 8½, 9)"
15½ (15½, 15½,15½, 15½, 15, 15, 15)"
FRONT & BACK
15½ (15½, 15½,15½, 15½, 15, 15, 15)"
7½ (8, 8½, 9, 9½, 10, 10½, 11)"
17 (18¼, 19¾, 20½, 21¾, 23, 24½, 26)"

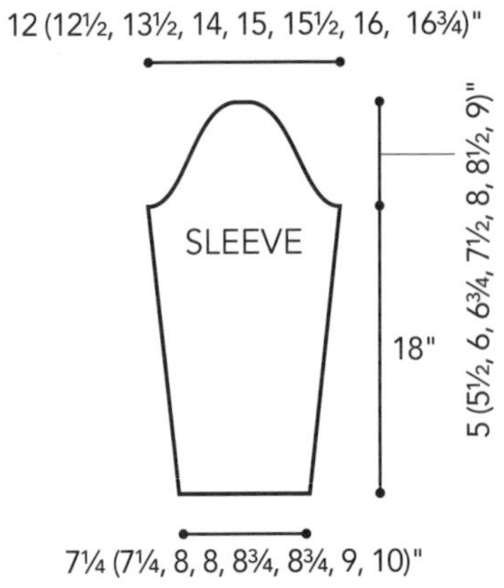
12 (12½, 13½, 14, 15, 15½, 16, 16¾)"
SLEEVE
18"
5 (5½, 6, 6¾, 7½, 8, 8½, 9)"
7¼ (7¼, 8, 8, 8¾, 8¾, 9, 10)"

●●○ Double-Seed-Stitch Pullover

Raglan sleeves and a ribbed mock turtleneck give classic details to this pullover.

SIZES
Sized for Small, Medium, Large, X-Large, XX-Large and shown in size Small.

KNITTED MEASUREMENTS
- Bust 38 (42, 45½, 49½, 54½)"/96.5 (106.5, 115.5, 125.5, 138.5)cm
- Length 21 (22, 23, 23½, 24)"/54 (56, 58.5, 60, 61)cm
- Upper arm 15 (16, 17, 19, 20)"/38 (40.5, 43, 48, 50.5)cm

MATERIALS
- 5 (6, 7, 8, 9) 7oz/200g skeins (each approx 110yd/100.5m) of HiKoo Skacel Collection *Zumie* (acrylic/wool/nylon) in #109 laurel
- A few yards of a smooth yarn in a lighter weight and similar color for seaming
- One pair size 13 (9mm) needles, OR SIZE TO OBTAIN GAUGE
- Size 13 (9mm) circular needle, 16"/40cm long

GAUGE
8½ sts and 13 rows = 4"/10cm over double seed stitch using size 13 (9mm) needles.
TAKE TIME TO CHECK GAUGE.

DOUBLE SEED STITCH
(odd number of sts)
Row 1 K1, *p1, k1; rep from * to end.
Row 2 P1, *k1, p1; rep from * to end.
Row 3 Rep row 2.
Row 4 Rep row 1.
Rep rows 1–4 for double seed st.

BACK
Cast on 41 (45, 49, 53, 59) sts.
Work in k1, p1 rib for 6 (6, 8, 8, 8) rows, end with a WS row.
Work in double seed st until piece measures 13½ (13½, 13¾, 13¾, 13¾)"/34.5 (34.5, 35, 35, 35)cm from beg, end with a WS row.

ARMHOLE SHAPING
Bind off 2 (3, 3, 3, 3) sts at beg of next 2 rows, 0 (0, 2, 2, 2) sts at beg of next 0 (0, 2, 2, 6) rows. Dec 1 st each side on next row then every other row 7 (8, 8, 9, 8) times more—21 (21, 21, 23, 23 sts.
Mark center 13 (13, 13, 15, 15) sts.

NECK SHAPING
Next row (RS) Ssk, work to center sts, join 2nd ball of yarn and bind off center 13 (13, 13, 15, 15) sts, work to last 2 sts, k2tog—3 sts rem each side.
Dec 1 st at each neck edge on next WS row—2 sts each side.
Last row (RS) SKP each side.
Fasten off last st each side.

FRONT
Work as for back to armhole shaping.

ARMHOLE SHAPING
Work same as back armhole shaping until there are 23 (23, 23, 25, 25) sts, end with a WS row.

NECK SHAPING
Mark center 11 (11, 11, 13, 13) sts.
Next row (RS) Ssk, work to marked sts, join 2nd ball of yarn and bind off center 11 (11, 11, 13, 13) sts, work to last 2 sts, k2tog—5 sts rem each side.
Work 1 row even.
Next row (RS) Dec 1 st at each armhole and each neck edge—3 sts rem each side.
Work 1 row even.
Last row (RS) SK2P and fasten off last st each side.

SLEEVES
Cast on 23 (23, 23, 25, 25) sts. Work in k1, p1 rib for 2½"/6.5cm, end with a WS row. Work in double seed st and inc 1 st each side, working inc sts into double seed st, every 8th (6th, 6th, 4th, 4th) row 5 (2, 5, 2, 5) times, then every 0 (8th, 8th, 6th, 6th) row 0 (4, 2, 6, 4) times—33 (35, 37, 41, 43) sts.
Work even until piece measures 18"/45cm from beg, end with a WS row.

CAP SHAPING
Bind off 2 (3, 3, 3, 3) sts at beg of next 2 rows, 0 (0, 2, 2, 2) sts at beg of next 0 (0, 2, 2, 6) rows. Dec 1 st each side every 4th row 0 (1, 2, 1, 3) times, then every other row 8 (7, 5, 8, 3) times, then every row twice—9 sts. Bind off.

FINISHING
Note For less bulky seams, use a smooth yarn in a lighter weight and similar color for seaming. Sew raglan seams.

NECKBAND
With RS facing and circular needle, beg at right back seam, pick up and k 20 (20, 20, 22, 22) sts along back, 8 sts along left sleeve, 20 (20, 20, 22, 22) sts along front, 8 sts along right sleeve—56 (56, 56, 60, 60) sts. Join and work in k1, p1 rib in rnds for 5"/12.5cm. Bind off loosely in rib.
Sew side and sleeve seams. ■

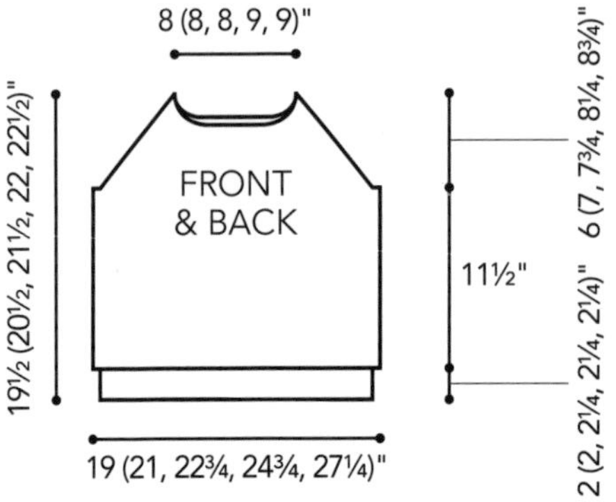
8 (8, 8, 9, 9)"
FRONT & BACK
19½ (20½, 21½, 22, 22½)"
11½"
6 (7, 7¾, 8¼, 8¾)"
2 (2, 2¼, 2¼, 2¼)"
19 (21, 22¾, 24¾, 27¼)"

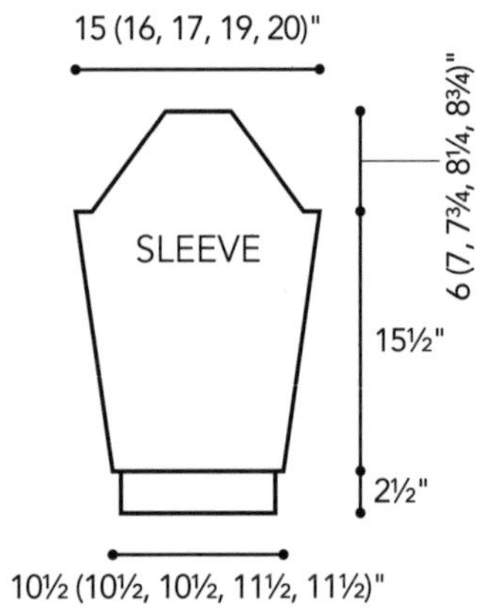
15 (16, 17, 19, 20)"
SLEEVE
6 (7, 7¾, 8¼, 8¾)"
15½"
2½"
10½ (10½, 10½, 11½, 11½)"

••• Garter & Cable Scarf

This long winter scarf, knitted in luxurious cashmere, is a great project for perfecting your garter stitch and practicing your cable knitting skills.

KNITTED MEASUREMENTS
- Width 7"/17.5cm
- Length approx 86"/218cm

MATERIALS
- 4 1.94oz/55g hanks (each approx 150yd/137m) of Jade Sapphire *Mongolian Cashmere* 6-Ply (cashmere) in #156 robe royale
- One pair size 6 (4mm) needles, OR SIZE TO OBTAIN GAUGE
- Cable needle (cn)
- Stitch markers

GAUGE
19 sts and 34 rows = 4"/10cm over garter st using size 6 (4mm) needles. TAKE TIME TO CHECK GAUGE.

STITCH GLOSSARY
4-st RC
Slip 2 sts to cn and hold to *back*, k2, k2 from cn.

4-st LC
Slip 2 sts to cn and hold to *front*, k2, k2 from cn.

SCARF
Cast on 34 sts.

BEG FIRST GARTER BLOCK
Row 1 Knit 33, sl 1 wyif.
Rep row 1 until there are 47 ridges, end with a WS row. Block measures approx 11"/28cm.

*BEG CABLE BLOCK
Inc row (RS) K3, place marker (pm), k3, kfb, k1, [p2, k6] twice, p2, k3, kfb, k1, pm, k2, sl 1 wyif—36 sts.
Row 1 and all WS rows K3, [p6, k2] 3 times, p6, k2, sl 1 wyif.
Row 2 K3, [4-st RC, k2, p2] 3 times, 4-st RC, k4, sl 1 wyif.
Row 4 K3, [k6, p2] 3 times, k8, sl 1 wyif.
Row 6 K3, [k2, 4-st LC, p2] 3 times, 4-st LC, k4, sl 1 wyif.
Row 8 Rep row 4. Rep rows 1–8 nine times more, then work row 1 once more. Cable block measures approx 14"/35.5cm.

BEG NEXT GARTER BLOCK
Dec row (RS) K6, k2tog, k to last 7 sts, k2tog, k4, sl 1 wyif—34 sts.
Row 1 Knit 33, sl 1 wyif. Rep row 1 until there are 47 ridges, end with a WS row. Block measures approx 11"/28cm. Rep from * twice more. Bind off.

FINISHING
Block lightly to measurements. ∎

••• Striped Hat & Scarf

Striped scarf and hat in garter and stockinette stitch. The scarf is worked long edge to long edge.

SIZE
Instructions are written for one size.

KNITTED MEASUREMENTS
• Scarf 9½ x 66"/224 x 167.5cm
• Hat circumference 21"/53cm

MATERIALS
• 2 1¾oz/50g balls (each approx 124yd/113m of Rowan Yarns *Yorkshire Tweed DK* (wool) in #351 black (A)

• 1 ball each in #349 green (B), #345 medium blue (C), #342 purple (D), #344 scarlet (E), #346 navy (F), #354 gray (G)

• Size 6 (4mm) needles
OR SIZE TO OBTAIN GAUGE

GAUGE
20 sts and 31 rows to 4"/10cm over St st using size 6 (4mm) needles.
TAKE TIME TO CHECK GAUGE.

SCARF
With A, cast on 330 sts. Knit 2 rows. Change to St st (k on RS, p on WS) and work the foll two 70-row stripe pats simultaneously by working section 1 over first 165 sts and section 2 over next 165 sts. Pm between 165th and 166th sts to mark center of row.

Section 1 (70 rows)
6 rows A, 6 B, 10 C, 1 D, 4 E, 3 D, 10 A, 10 B, 12 F, 1 E, 7 G.

Section 2 (70 rows)
10 rows A, 17 B, 2 G, 14 E, 8 A, 10 F, 2 B, 7 F.

When 70-row stripe pat has been completed, change to A and knit 2 rows. Bind off.

EDGING
With RS facing and D, pick up and k 48 sts evenly spaced along one short edge of scarf. Work even in garter st for 3 rows. Bind off. Rep edging on opposite short edge of scarf.

HAT
SIDES OF HAT
With A, cast on 105 sts. Work 6 rows St st (k on RS, p on WS) and 6 rows garter st (k every row). Change to F and work 6 rows St st. Cont as foll:
4 rows D in garter st, 6 rows B in St st,
4 rows D in garter st, 6 rows G in St st,
4 rows D in garter st, 6 rows F in St st,
4 rows D in St st, 2 rows A in garter st.
Bind off.

CROWN
With A, cast on 32 sts. Work in St st and shape crown in short rows as foll:
Row 1 K24, turn, leaving rem sts unworked.
Row 2 P16, turn.
Row 3 K17, turn.
Row 4 P18, turn.
Cont in this way to work 1 more st on each row until all 32 sts are being worked. Mark each end of 32-st row. Work even until piece measures 9"/23cm from beg. Mark each end of last row for center of crown. Make a note of the measurement between the row markers. Work even until piece measures noted measurement from 2nd set of markers, end with a WS row. Shape crown in short rows as foll:
Row 1 K31, turn.
Row 2 P30, turn. Cont to work 1 less st on each row in this way until p16 is worked.
Next row Work across all 32 sts. Bind off.

FINISHING
Sew side seam. With A, sew crown to top edge on WS of work. With A, and RS of crown facing, fold sides of hat at D garter st rows and sew a line of running sts through both thicknesses approx ½"/1.5cm from edge of crown, thereby creating a "shelf" around the crown.
Tie 2 strands of E and one strand of D together and make a 2"/5cm braid; knot the end and trim to so piece measures 3"/7.5cm in total. Sew braid at center of crown. ■

●●● Pull-Through Wrap

An oversized garter-stitch wrap with contrasting color ribbing at the side edges and a keyhole opening for crossing the ends.

KNITTED MEASUREMENTS
• Width 23½"/60cm
• Length 79"/200cm

MATERIALS
• 6 4oz/113g skeins (each approx 190yd/174m) of Brown Sheep *Lamb's Pride Worsted* (wool/mohair) in #M03 gray heather (MC)

• 1 skein each in #M120 limeade (A) and #M38 lotus pink (B)

• One pair size 8 (5mm) needles OR SIZE TO OBTAIN GAUGE

• Stitch holders

GAUGE
16 sts and 30 rows = 4"/10cm over garter st using size 8 (5mm) needles. TAKE TIME TO CHECK GAUGE.

NOTES
1 Knit first and last st of every row for garter st selvage.
2 When changing colors, twist yarns on WS to prevent holes in work.

WRAP
With B cast on 8 sts, with MC cast on 80 sts, with A cast on 8 sts—96 sts. You will have three different yarns on your cast-on needle.

BEG PAT
Row 1 (RS) With A, k1 (selvage st), [p2, k1] twice, p1; with MC k80; with B, p1, [k1, p2] twice, k1 (selvage st).
Row 2 (WS) With B, k1 (selvage st), [k2, p1] twice, k1; with MC k80; with A, k1, [p1, k2] twice, k1 (selvage st).
Rep rows 1 and 2 for pat until piece measures 23½"/60cm from beg.

BEG KEYHOLE OPENING
Next row (RS) Keeping to pat, work 48 sts and place these sts on a st holder, work rem 48 sts in pat to end of row.
Cont in pat over 48 sts on needle until piece measures 4"/10cm from opening, end with a WS row. Place sts on a 2nd st holder. Slip sts from first holder to needle to work next row from WS and work in pat over these 48 sts until same number of rows as first side have been worked, ending with a WS row.
Joining row (RS) Work 48 sts on needle, then work 48 sts from 2nd holder—96 sts.
Cont in pat as established until piece measures 79"/200cm from beg, end with a WS row. Bind off knitwise on RS, matching colors.

FINISHING
Block piece to measurements. ■

●●● Slouchy Hat

Knit up this easy-to-wear slouchy hat in alternating bands of twisted rib and fisherman's rib.

FINISHED MEASUREMENTS
• Brim circumference (unstretched) 18"/45.5cm
• Length 10"/25.5cm

MATERIALS
ORIGINAL YARN
• 3 1¾oz/50g balls (each approx 93yd/85m) of Kolláge Yarns *Fantastic* (wool) in #7506 magenta

SUBSTITUTE YARN
• 3 1¾oz/50g balls (each approx 97yd/88m) of Valley Yarns *Valley Superwash* (wool) in #302 sriracha

• One each sizes 6 and 7 (4 and 4.5mm) circular needles each 16"/40cm long, OR SIZE TO OBTAIN GAUGE

• One set (5) size 7 (4.5mm) double-pointed needles (dpns)

• Stitch markers

GAUGE
22 sts and 36 rnds = 4"/10cm over 8 rnds twisted rib alternating with 8 rnds fisherman's rib using size 7 (4.5mm) needle.
TAKE TIME TO CHECK GAUGE.

STITCH GLOSSARY
k1b Knit 1 in the row below.
p1b Purl 1 in the row below.

TWISTED RIB
(multiple of 2 sts)
Rnd 1 *K1tbl, p1;
rep from * to end of rnd.
Rnd 2 *K1, p1tbl;
rep from * to end of rnd.
Rep rnds 1 and 2 for twisted rib.

FISHERMAN'S RIB
(multiple of 2 sts)
Rnd 1 *K1b, p1; rep from * to end of rnd.
Rnd 2 *K1, p1b; rep from * to end of rnd.
Rep rnds 1 and 2 for fisherman's rib.

HAT
With smaller circular needle, cast on 100 sts. Join, taking care not to twist sts, and place marker (pm) for beg of rnd. Work in twisted rib for 1¾"/4.5cm, end with a rnd 2. Change to larger circular needle. Work in fisherman's rib for 8 rnds. [Work 8 rnds in twisted rib, 8 rnds in fisherman's rib] 3 times, placing markers every 10 sts on last rnd.

SHAPE CROWN
Note Change to dpns when sts no longer fit comfortably on circular needle.
Working in twisted rib pat, work as foll:
Dec rnd 1 [K2tog tbl, work in rib as established to next marker] 10 times—10 sts dec'd.
Dec rnd 2 [Ssk, work in rib as established to next marker] 10 times—10 sts dec'd.
Rep last 2 rnds 3 times more—20 sts.
Next rnd [K2tog tbl] 10 times—10 sts.
Cut yarn and thread through rem sts, draw up tightly and secure.

FINISHING
Pompom
Make a 4"/10cm pompom and secure to top of hat. ■

••• Mohair Cardigan

A very oversized cardigan in loose-knit stockinette stitch with self-finished front bands.

SIZES
Sized for Small, Medium, Large, X-Large, 1X and shown in size Medium.

KNITTED MEASUREMENTS
• Bust (closed) 54 (57, 60, 63, 66)"/137 (144.5, 152, 160, 167.5)cm
• Length 22 (22½, 23, 23½, 24)"/56 (57, 58.5, 59.5, 61)cm
• Upper arm 12 (13, 14, 15, 16)"/30.5 (33, 35.5, 38, 40.5)cm

MATERIALS
• 5 (6, 6, 7, 7) 1¾oz/50g balls (each approx 222yd/203m) of Be Sweet *Medium Brushed Mohair* (kid mohair/wool/acrylic) in #20 natural

• One pair each sizes 13 and 15 (9 and 10mm) needles,
OR SIZE TO OBTAIN GAUGE

• Removable stitch markers

• Six 1-inch/25mm buttons

GAUGE
10 sts and 13 rows = 4"/10cm over St st using 2 strands of yarn held tog and larger needles.
TAKE TIME TO CHECK GAUGE.

NOTES
1 Cardigan is worked using 2 strands of yarn held tog throughout.
2 One selvage st is worked each side and is not figured into the finished measurements.

BACK
With smaller needles and 2 strands of yarn held tog, cast on 57 (61, 65, 69, 73) sts.
Row 1 (RS) K1, *p1, k1; rep from * to end.
Row 2 P1, *k1, p1; rep from * to end.
Rep these 2 rows once more for k1, p1 rib.
Change to larger needles.
Then, cont in St st (k on RS, p on WS) for 6 rows.
Inc row (RS) K3, M1, k to last 3 sts, M1, k3—2 sts inc'd.
Rep inc row every 6th row 5 times more—69 (73, 77, 81, 85) sts.
Work even until piece measures 14½"/37cm from beg.
Pm each side of last row worked to mark for sleeve at armhole.
Work even until piece measures 6 (6½, 7, 7½, 8)"/15 (16.5, 18, 19, 20.5)cm from the markers, and on the last WS row, pm to mark the center 19 sts on the last WS row.

SHOULDER SHAPING
Next row (RS) Bind off 9 (9, 9, 11, 11) sts, k to center marked sts, sl marker, work p1, [k1, p1] 9 times, sl marker, k to end.
Next row (WS) Bind off 9 (9, 9, 11, 11) sts, p to center marked sts, sl marker, k1, [p1, k1] 9 times, sl marker, p to end.
Cont to bind off 8 (9, 10, 10, 11) sts at beg of next 4 rows, AT SAME TIME, work the sts between markers in established rib pat and bind off these 19 sts on last row.

LEFT FRONT
With smaller needles and 2 strands of yarn held tog, cast on 29 (31, 33, 35, 37) sts.
Row 1 (RS) *K1, p1; rep from *, end k1.
Row 2 Sl 1, *k1, p1; rep from * to end.
Rep these 2 rows once more.
Change to larger needles.
Row 1 (RS) K23 (25, 27, 29, 31), [p1, k1] 3 times.
Row 2 (WS) Sl 1, k1, [p1, k1] twice, purl to end.
Rep these 2 rows for St st, with 6-st front band, for 4 rows more.
Inc row (RS) K3, M1, work to end.
Rep inc row every 6th row 5 times more—35 (37, 39, 41, 43) sts.
Work even for 17 rows more or until piece measures approx 17"/43cm from beg, AT SAME TIME, pm at armhole edge when same length as back.

NECK SHAPING
Dec row (RS) K to last 8 sts, k2tog, rib 6.
Rep dec row every other row 9 times more, AT SAME TIME, when piece measures same as back to shoulder, work shoulder shaping by binding off 9 (9, 9, 11, 11) sts from shoulder edge once, then 8 (9, 10, 10, 11) sts twice.

RIGHT FRONT
With smaller needles and 2 strands of yarn held tog, cast on 29 (31, 33, 35, 37) sts.
Row 1 (RS) Sl 1, *p1, k1; rep from * to end.
Row 2 P1, *k1, p1; rep from * to end.
Buttonhole row 3 (RS) Sl 1, p1, k2tog, yo (for buttonhole), rib to end.
Row 4 Rep row 2.
Change to larger needles.
Next row (RS) Rib 6, k to end.

Cont in St st, with the 6-st band, for 5 rows more.

Note Read before cont to knit.
Inc row (RS) K to last 3 sts, end M1, k3.
Rep inc row every 6th row 5 times more, AT SAME TIME, after 1 row is worked after the inc row, rep buttonhole row on the next RS row, then rep buttonhole row every 10th row 4 times more.
When 1 row is worked even after the last buttonhole, work as foll:

NECK SHAPING
Dec row (RS) Rib 6, k2tog, k to end.
Rep this dec row every other row 9 times more, AT SAME TIME, shape shoulder as for left front when same length as back.

SLEEVES
With smaller needles and 2 strands of yarn held tog, cast on 23 (25, 27, 29, 31) sts.
Work in k1, p1 rib as on back for 4 rows, inc 0 (0, 0, 1, 1) st on last WS row—23 (25, 27, 30, 32) sts.
Change to larger needles.
Then, cont in St st for 6 rows.
Inc row (RS) K3, M1, k to last 3 sts, end M1, k3—2 sts inc'd.
Rep inc row every 8th row 4 times more—33 (35, 37, 40, 42) sts.
Work even until piece measures 17"/43cm from beg.

FINISHING
Bind off. ∎

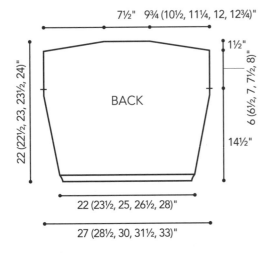

BACK

7½" 9¾ (10½, 11¼, 12, 12¾)"
1½"
6 (6½, 7, 7½, 8)"
14½"
22 (22½, 23, 23½, 24)"
22 (23½, 25, 26½, 28)"
27 (28½, 30, 31½, 33)"

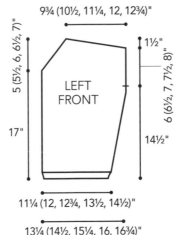

LEFT FRONT

9¾ (10½, 11¼, 12, 12¾)"
5 (5½, 6, 6½, 7)"
1½"
6 (6½, 7, 7½, 8)"
17"
14½"
11¼ (12, 12¾, 13½, 14½)"
13¼ (14½, 15¼, 16, 16¾)"

SLEEVE

12 (13, 14, 15, 16)"
17"
8½ (9¼, 10, 10¾, 11½)"

••• Cropped Eyelet Pullover

Oversized cropped pullover in an eyelet pattern, with three-quarter sleeves and a wide neck.

SIZES
Sized for Small, Medium, Large, X-Large and shown in size Small.

KNITTED MEASUREMENTS
• Bust 40 (44, 48, 52)"/101.5 (111.5, 122, 132)cm
• Length 17 (17½, 20, 20½)"/43 (44.5, 50.5, 52)cm
• Upper arm 14 (14, 16, 16)"/36 (36, 40, 40)cm

MATERIALS
• 5 (6, 6, 7) 3½oz/100g hanks (each approx 127yd/116m) of Ancient Art Yarns *Big Squeeze Bulky* (wool) in Irish linen
• One pair size 9 (5.5mm) needles, OR SIZE TO OBTAIN GAUGE
• Size 8 (5mm) circular needle, 24"/60cm long
• Stitch markers
• Stitch holders

GAUGE
12 sts and 21 rows = 4"/10cm over eyelet pattern using larger needles. TAKE TIME TO CHECK GAUGE.

EYELET PATTERN
(multiple of 6 sts plus 7)
Row 1 (RS) Sl 1 wyif, k1, *k3, yo, k3tog, yo; rep from * to last 5 sts, k5.
Row 2 Sl 1 wyif, k1, purl to last 2 sts, k2.
Row 3 Sl 1 wyif, k1, *yo, k3tog, yo, k3; rep from * to last 5 sts, yo, k3tog, yo, k2.
Row 4 Rep row 2.
Rep rows 1–4 for eyelet pat.

BACK
With larger needles cast on 61 (67, 73, 79) sts.
Set-up row (WS) Sl 1 wyif, k1, purl to last 2 sts, k2.
Work in eyelet pat until piece measures 17 (17½, 20, 20½)"/43 (44.5, 50.5, 52)cm, end with a RS row.

Next row (WS) Work 18 (21, 23, 26) sts in pat and place sts on a st holder, bind off center 25 (25, 27, 27) sts for back neck, work in pat to end and place rem 18 (21, 23, 26) sts on a st holder.

FRONT

Work as for back until piece measures 14 (14½, 15½, 16)"/36 (37, 39.5, 40.5)cm from beg, end with a WS row.

NECK SHAPING

Next row (RS) Work 27 (30, 32, 35) sts in pat, join 2nd ball of yarn and bind off center 7 (7, 9, 9) sts for neck, work to end. Working both sides at once, bind off from each neck edge 2 sts once, then dec 1 st at each neck edge every row 7 times. Work even on rem 18 (21, 23, 26) sts each side until same length as back. Place sts each side on st holders.

SLEEVES

With larger needles cast on 43 (43, 49, 49) sts.
Set-up row (WS) Sl 1 wyif, k1, purl to last 2 sts, k2.
Work in eyelet pat until piece measures 11½ (12, 12, 12½)"/29 (30.5, 30.5, 31.5)cm from beg, end with a WS row.

CAP SHAPING

Bind off 3 sts at beg of next 2 rows, 2 sts at beg of next 2 rows. Dec 1 st each side every row 7 (7, 10, 10) times. Bind off rem 19 sts.

FINISHING

Block pieces to measurements. Join shoulder seams using 3-needle bind off. Place markers 9 (9, 10, 10)"/23 (23, 25.5, 25.5)cm down from shoulder seams on front and back for armholes. With center of top of sleeve at shoulder seam, sew sleeve cap between markers, easing in to fit. Sew side and sleeve seams.

NECKBAND

With RS facing and circular needle, pick up and k 88 (88, 92, 92) sts evenly around neck edge. Join and place marker for beg of rnd.
Next rnd *K1, p1; rep from * around. Rep last rnd for k1, p1 rib for ½"/1.5cm. Bind off knitwise. ■

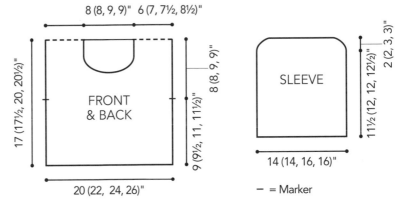

8 (8, 9, 9)" 6 (7, 7½, 8½)"

17 (17½, 20, 20½)"

FRONT & BACK

8 (8, 9, 9)"

9 (9½, 11, 11½)"

20 (22, 24, 26)"

SLEEVE

11½ (12, 12, 12½)"

2 (2, 3, 3)"

14 (14, 16, 16)"

— = Marker

●●● Bucket Hat

Loose-fitting bucket-style hat with stockinette-stitch crown and garter-stitch brim in contrasting colors.

SIZE
Instructions are written for one size.

KNITTED MEASUREMENTS
Circumference 18"/45.5cm

MATERIALS
• 2 3½oz/100g hanks
(each approx 100yd/91m) of Blue Sky Fibers *Worsted Hand Dyes* (alpaca/merino wool) in #2015 putty (A)

• 1 hank in #2016 chocolate (B)

• One each size 9 (5.5mm) circular needles, 16"/40cm and 24"/60cm long, OR SIZE TO OBTAIN GAUGE

• One extra size 9 (5.5mm) needle

• 20"/51cm long, ½"/12.5mm wide elastic

• Stitch marker

GAUGES
• 12 sts and 16 rows = 4"/10cm over garter st with 2 strands of yarn held tog.

• 16 sts and 20 rows = 4"/10cm over St st with 1 strand of yarn.
TAKE TIME TO CHECK GAUGES.

BRIM
With 2 strands of A held tog and longer circular needle, cast on 96 sts. Place marker and join for knitting in the round, taking care not to twist sts. [Purl 1 rnd, knit 1 rnd] twice, purl 1 rnd.
Dec rnd 1 *K10, k2tog; rep from *around—88 sts. Purl 1 rnd.
Dec rnd 2 K5, *k2tog, k9; rep from *to last 6 sts, k2tog, k4—80 sts. Purl 1 rnd, knit 1 rnd, purl 1 rnd.
Dec rnd 3 *K8, k2tog; rep from *around—72 sts. Purl 1 rnd, knit 1 rnd, purl 1 rnd.
Dec rnd 4 K4, *k2tog, k7; rep from * to last 5 sts, k2tog, k3—64 sts. Purl 1 rnd, knit 1 rnd, purl 1 rnd.
Dec rnd 5 *K6, k2tog; rep from * around—56 sts. Purl 1 rnd, knit 1 rnd, purl 1 rnd.
Dec rnd 6 K3, *k2tog, k5; rep from * to last 4 sts, k2tog, k2—48 sts. Purl 1 rnd, knit 1 rnd, purl 1 rnd.

CROWN
Change to shorter circular needle and single strand of B, and work in St st as foll:
Next (inc) rnd *K1, inc 1 st in next st; rep from *around—72 sts. Knit 4 rnds even. Leave sts on circular needle.

CASING
Turn hat WS facing, with longer circular needle and single strand of B, pick up and k 72 sts at border of brim and crown.
Note Do not join. This will form slit for elastic. Work 3 rows in St st.
With RS facing and shorter circular needle, knit tog 1 st from each needle, closing casing. Work even until crown measures 7"/18cm.

FINISHING
Next rnd Work 36 sts. Turn inside out. Place last 36 sts on extra needle. Bind off all sts using 3-needle bind-off. Turn hat right side out, sew corners of top together. Thread elastic through casing and adjust to fit. ∎

••• Gradient Wrap

A rectangle wrap is worked in a rib-and-garter block stitch.

KNITTED MEASUREMENTS
- Width 18"/45.5cm
- Length 68"/172.5cm

MATERIALS
- 3 7oz/200g balls (each approx 437yd/400m) of Hikoo/Skacel Collection *Concentric* (baby alpaca) in #1033 classically trained
- One pair size 8 (5mm) needles, OR SIZE TO OBTAIN GAUGE

GAUGE
24 sts and 27 rows = 4"/10cm over block stitch pattern using size 8 (5mm) needles.
TAKE TIME TO CHECK GAUGE.

NOTE
To achieve the gradient striping as seen in the sample, work from the center of the first ball to the end, from the outside of the 2nd ball to the end, then work from the center of the third ball until the 68"/172.5cm length is achieved.

WRAP
Cast on 108 sts.
Row 1 (RS) *K1, [p1, k1] 4 times, k9; rep from * 5 times more.
Row 2 (WS) *K9, p1, [k1, p1] 4 times; rep from * 5 times more.
Rows 3, 5, 7 and 9 Rep row 1.
Rows 4, 6, 8 and 10 Rep row 2.

Row 11 (RS) *K9, k1, [p1, k1] 4 times; rep from * 5 times more.
Row 12 (WS) *P1, [k1, p1] 4 times, k9; rep from * 5 times more.
Rows 13, 15, 17 and 19 Rep row 11.
Rows 14, 16, 18 and 20 Rep row 12.
Rep rows 1–20 for block stitch pattern 21 times more, then rep rows 1–19 once more. Piece measures approx 68"/172.5cm from beg. Bind off in pat on WS.

FINISHING
Do *not* block the finished piece.
Weave in with the ends split and worked in different directions. ∎

••• Placket-Neckline Poncho

Very oversized poncho in double strand of two colors for a marled effect with a pleat-front placket and open sides.

SIZES
Sized for Small/Medium, Large/X-Large, XX-Large and shown in size Small/Medium.

KNITTED MEASUREMENTS
• Bust 77 (79, 81)"/195.5 (200.5, 205.5)cm
• Length 25¾ (26¼, 26¾)"/65.5 (66.5, 68)cm
• Upper arm 9 (10, 11)"/23 (25.5, 28)cm

MATERIALS
• 17 (18, 19) 1¾oz/50g balls (each approx 95yd/87m) of Sugar Bush Yarns *Crisp* (wool) each in #2018 titanium (light gray–A) and #2019 lead (dark gray–B)
• One each sizes 9 and 10 (5.5 and 6mm) circular needle, each 29"/74cm long OR SIZE TO OBTAIN GAUGE
• One set (4) size 10 (6mm) double-pointed needles (dpn)
• Stitch holders
• Stitch markers

GAUGE
15 sts and 23 rows = 4"/10cm over St st using 1 strand each of A and B held tog and larger needles.
TAKE TIME TO CHECK GAUGE.

STITCH GLOSSARY
Ssp With yarn in front, slip 2 sts knitwise, one at a time, to right-hand needle. Insert tip of left-hand needle into backs of these sts, from left to right, and purl them together.

PURL GARTER RIB
(over an odd number of sts)
Row 1 (RS) K1, *p1, k1; rep from * to end.
Row 2 Purl.
Rep these 2 rows for purl garter rib.

NOTES
1) Work with 1 strand each of A and B held tog throughout.
2) Poncho is worked flat. Circular needles are used to accommodate large number of stitches.

BACK
With smaller needle and 1 strand each of A and B held tog, cast on 147 (151, 155) sts. Work in purl garter rib until piece measures 3"/7.5cm from beg, end with a WS row. Change to larger needle.

BEG BODY
Row 1 (RS) [K1, p1] 3 times, k to the last 6 sts, [p1, k1] 3 times.
Row 2 Purl.
Rep these 2 rows for St st with 6-st rib borders each side until piece measures 25 (25½, 26)"/63.5 (65, 66)cm from beg, end with a WS row.

NECK SHAPING
Next row (RS) Rib 6, k58 (60, 62), sl center 19 sts to a st holder, join two new strands of yarn held tog and k58 (60, 62), rib 6. Working both sides at once, bind off 5 sts from each neck edge twice. Bind off rem 54 (56, 58) sts each side.

FRONT
Note: The front is wider than the back at the lower edge to accommodate the pleated placket at the center front neck edge.
With smaller needle and 1 strand A and B held tog, cast on 155 (159, 163) sts.

Work same as for back through the rib border. Work row 1 of the body and inc 1 st at the center—156 (160, 164) sts.

Work even until piece measures 16 (16½, 17)"/40.5 (42, 43)cm from beg, end with a WS row.

PLACKET SET-UP
Next row (RS) Rib 6, k64 (66, 68), then sl the next 8 sts to dpn and hold these sts at back of work and parallel to the next sts on the circular needle, [k1 from circular needle at front tog with 1 st from dpn at back] 8 times for the pleat, k64 (66, 68), rib 6.
Next row (WS) Purl.

DIVIDE FOR NECK OPENING
Next row (RS) Work 70 (72, 74) sts, join 2 new strands of yarn held tog and bind off center 8 sts, work to end. Work both sides at once for 6"/15cm.

NECK SHAPING
Working both sides at once, bind off 4 sts from each neck edge once, 3 sts once, then 2 sts once.
Dec row 1 (RS) First side: Work to the last 3 sts, k2tog, k1; on 2nd side, k1, ssk, work to end.
Dec row 2 (WS) First side: Work to last 3 sts, ssp, p1; on 2nd side, p1, p2tog, work to end.
Rep last 2 rows twice more, then rep dec row 1 once more—54 (56, 58) sts each side. Work even until there are same number of rows as back to shoulder.
Bind off rem sts each side for shoulders.

SLEEVES
With smaller needle and 1 strand A and B held tog, cast on 45 (51, 55) sts.
Row 1 (RS) K1, *p1; rep from * to end.
Row 2 P1, *k1, p1; rep from * to end.
Rep last 2 rows for k1, p1 rib for 4"/10cm.
Bind off in rib.

FINISHING
Sew shoulder seams.
Pm at 4½ (5, 5½)"/11.5 (12.5, 14)cm down from shoulders on back and front. Sew the bound-off edge of sleeves between markers. Note that the rem of the side edges of the poncho are left open so that the entire edge forms a long side slit.

PLACKET TRIM
With RS facing, smaller needle and 1 strand A and B held tog, pick up and k 21 sts along the left front placket edge. Work in k1, p1 rib as on sleeves for 9 rows. Bind off in rib. Work the right front neck edge placket trim in same way. Sew the placket trims to center front, sewing the right front edge overlapping the left front at the center.

COLLAR
With RS facing, smaller needle and 1 strand A and B held tog, pick up and k 7 sts from right placket trim, 26 sts from shaped front neck edge, 13 sts from shaped back neck edge, 19 sts from back neck holder, 13 sts from shaped back neck edge, 33 sts from left front neck as for right front—111 sts. Work in k1, p1 rib as on sleeves for 9 rows.
Bind off in rib.
Block lightly on the WS avoiding the rib edges. ■

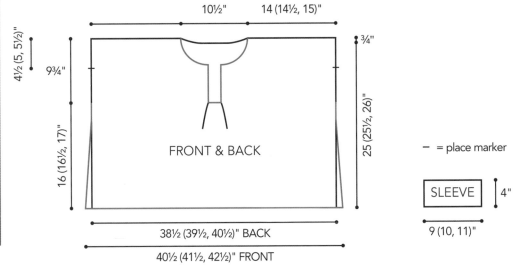

Index

INDEX *(side tab)*